OSPREY AIRCRAFT OF THE ACES • 4

Korean War Aces

SERIES EDITOR: TONY HOLMES

OSPREY AIRCRAFT OF THE ACES • 4

Korean War Aces

Robert F Dorr, Jon Lake
and Warren Thompson

OSPREY
AEROSPACE

First published in Great Britain in 1995
by Osprey, an imprint of Reed Consumer Books Limited
Michelin House, 81 Fulham Road,
London SW3 6RB
and Auckland, Melbourne, Singapore and Toronto

ISBN 1 85532 501 2

Edited by Tony Holmes
Page design by TT Designs, Tony Truscott & Stuart Truscott

Cover Artwork by Iain Wyllie
Aircraft Profiles by Chris Davey and John Weal
Figure Artwork by Mike Chappell
Scale Drawings by Mark Styling

Printed in Hong Kong

ACKNOWLEDGEMENTS
The editor duly acknowledges the help given to the artists by Larry Davis, and would
like to thank Jerry Scutts, Tony Fairbairn and Richard Riding for furnishing
additional photographs.

EDITOR'S NOTE
To make this new series as authoritative as possible, the editor would be extremely
interested in hearing from any individual who may have relevant photographs,
documentation or first-hand experiences relating to the elite pilots, and their aircraft,
of the various theatres of war. Any material used will be fully credited to its original
source.

ARTIST'S NOTE
Readers may care to note that the original figure paintings from which the colour
plates in this book were prepared are available for private sale. All reproduction
copyright whatsoever is retained by the publisher.
All enquiries should be addressed to:
Mike Chappell, 19 Downlands, Walmer, Kent, CT14 7XT
The publishers regret that they can enter into no correspondence upon
this matter.

Front cover
**Second ranking USAF ace in Korea
with 15 kills, Maj James Jabara goes
head-to-head with a formation of 16
MiGs at high altitude over Uiju on 26
May 1953. On this day he was
leading a four-ship of F-86Fs of the
334th FIS/4th FIW on a patrol along
MiG Alley when he spotted the large
communist formation crossing the
Yalu. Without hesitating, he
immediately engaged the Russian
jets head-on, scattering the silver
fighters all over the sky. Jabara
claimed two kills from this mission –
one jet he shot down whilst the
other went into an uncontrollable
flick roll attempting to evade Jabara
aggressive collision course attack.
These were his eight and ninth
victories of the war (cover painting
by Iain Wyllie)**

CONTENTS

FR🙾M PR🙾PS TO JETS

Before daybreak on Sunday, 25 June 1950, amid squalls of rain, North Korean forces invaded South Korea with 90,000 men and hundreds of Russian-made T-34 tanks. Aerial support for the invasion took the form of 150 prop-driven combat aircraft, including Lavochkin La-7s, Ilyushin Il-10 Sturmoviks and Yakovlev Yak-3s, -7s, -9s and -18s. Also reported, possibly in error, were North Koreans flying Bell F-63 Kingcobras, 2456 of which had gone to the USSR under Lend-Lease six years before.

The principal American fighter in the Far East at the time was the F-80C Shooting Star. The USAF's Far East Air Forces (FEAF) HQ was sited in Tokyo, and commanded by Lt Gen George E Stratemeyer. Maj Gen Earle E Partridge, of FEAF's Fifth Air Force, had at his disposal the 8th Fighter-Bomber Wing (FBW) (F-80Cs) at Itazuke, Japan, augmented by the 68th Fighter All-Weather Squadron (F(AW)S) (F-82 Twin Mustangs). At Misawa was the 49th FBW with F-80Cs, whilst located near to Tokyo at Yokota was the 339th F(AW)S with F-82s. On Okinawa was the 51st Fighter-Interceptor Wing (FIW) (F-80Cs), augmented by the 4th F(AW)S (F-82s). B-29s were nearby on Guam.

The closest aircraft carrier was USS *Valley Forge* (CVA-45), sailing near Hong Kong, with fighter squadrons VF-51 and -52 with F9F-3 Panthers and VF-53 and -54 with F4U-4B Corsairs embarked. A second carrier, USS *Philippine Sea* (CVA-47), was also steaming towards the war zone.

On the day of the invasion, US Ambassador to South Korea, John J Muccio, cabled Washington to tell them that four North Korean Yak-9 fighters had just strafed Seoul's Kimpo airport – he pleaded for 'positive and speedy action'.

President Harry S Truman at first authorised the use of force only to protect the evacuation of American citizens. On 26 June, F-82G Twin Mustangs were despatched from Itazuke to patrol the Seoul/Inchon area.

North Korea began the attack on its southern neighbour on 25 June 1950 with an air force consisting of about 150 propeller-driven combat aircraft, including Lavochkin La-9s, Ilyushin Il-10 *Sturmoviks* and Yakovlev Yak-7s, -9s and -18s. Typical was this Il-10, a heavy, robustly-armoured, Soviet veteran of the final days of fighting in World War 2. A significant number of Lavochkins, Ilyushins and Yaks were swept from the skies by United Nations F-80s and F-82s in the first hours of fighting. Weeks later, when the fortunes of war had reversed and Allied troops were overrunning North Korean airfields, this Il-10 was captured, along with two others. The trio were dissected at Cornell Aero Lab in Buffalo, New York, and flight-tested by the USAF at Wright-Patterson AFB, Ohio *(Cornell Aero Lab)*

Although it wasn't the principal USAF fighter in the Far East – that honour belonged to the F-80C Shooting Star – the F-82G Twin Mustang nevertheless equipped three squadrons in the FEAF when the Korean War began on 25 June 1950. Early Twin Mustangs had been flown by two pilots – a ludicrous arrangement – throughout the Air Force, but the radar-equipped F-82G nightfighter carried a radar operator in the right-hand seat instead. This F-82G (46-383) of the 68th F(AW)S, piloted by Lt William 'Skeeter' Hudson, with Lt Carl Fraser as radar observer (RO), shot down a Yak-7U on 27 June 1950, thus officially achieving the first aerial victory of the war. This historic machine was photographed whilst transiting over Japan, en route to North Korea, in December 1950 – note the red star kill marking below the closest cockpit *(Samuel Goldstein)*

Another F-82 unit within the FEAF that saw action over Korea in the first weeks of the campaign was the 4th F(AW)S, based at Naha, on Okinawa. This machine, nicknamed *Call Girl*, belonged to the unit's CO, Lt Col John Sharp *(Cecil Marshall)*

On one of their first patrols, two F-82s from the 68th F(AW)S were approached by La-7 fighters. Lt William 'Skeeter' Hudson ordered his element to drop external fuel tanks and turn into the North Korean warplanes. The communist pilots responded to this aggressive move by opening fire from too far out, and having badly missed the F-82s, they broke away. The first air-to-air engagement of the Korean War had ended with no real contact having been made.

The next day, however, brought no fewer than six aerial victories, equally shared by F-80s and F-82s. USAF pilots were to score 20 kills in 21 days (ending on 20 July), with their Navy brethren adding two more. No further victories would then be toted up until November 1950 after the Inchon invasion had reversed the tide, and the Allies marched north.

ENTER THE F-82

On 27 June 1950, North Korean fighters swarmed over Kimpo airfield. Maj James W 'Poke' Little, commander of the F-82G-equipped 339th F(AW)S, was one of the pilots in the air that day. The 4th and 339th had augmented the 68th at Itazuke, thereby producing the largest F-82 force ever mustered – all of 20 to 22 aircraft!

'Poke' Little had already become an ace flying with the 75th Fighter Squadron, 23rd Fighter Group – lineal descendants of the AVG's 'Flying Tigers' – in the China-Burma-India Theatre in World War 2. He had been credited with seven victories comprising six Zero fighters and one unidentified bomber, and now he was about to add another air-to-air kill to his Form Five, or flying record, but not just yet. Maj Little is credited with firing the first shot from an American gun in the Korean War, but is not, however, one of the two contenders for first aerial victory.

Lt Hudson and Lt Carl Fraser went into action in their Twin Mustang 46-383, nicknamed *BUCKET O' BOLTS*, of the 68th F(AW)S. Assigned a defensive mission over Kimpo airfield for the second day in a row, Hudson and Fraser shot down a two-seat Yak-7U. This success is usually cited as the first aerial victory of the Korean War, but Twin Mustang pilot, 1st Lt Charles B Moran, could have been first.

Radar observer Fraser recalls *BUCKET O' BOLTS* engagement. 'We were circling over Kimpo when two North Korean fighters came up out of some low clouds and started after Charlie Moran and Fred Larkins, who were flying in the number four F-82G in our flight. The North Koreans' shooting was a little better than yesterday and they shot up Charlie's tail.

'My pilot, "Skeeter" Hudson,

F-82G 46-357 was the aircraft flown by 1st Lt Charles Moran when he racked up one of three Twin Mustang kills against North Korean prop-driven fighters on 27 June 1950. Moran's F-82 did not escape the encounter without damage, however, and this snapshot illustrates the hits it took in the tail from the attacking North Korean pilot in a Lavochkin fighter. To the men who were on the scene it will never be certain which of three F-82 pilots – 'Skeeter' Hudson, 'Poke' Little or Charlie Moran – achieved the very first aerial victory of the Korean conflict *(via Tom Ivie)*

Although B*ucket O' Bolts* was the mount used by Fraser and Hudson to down their Yak, it wasn't their 'name' aircraft – that honour rested with this suitably customised F-82G. By the time this detail shot was taken in the autumn of 1950, 'Skeeter' Hudson had made captain *(Carl Fraser)*

slipped around and got on the tail of their flight leader. When he realised that we were there, he pulled up into some clouds and tried to shake us off. Fortunately, we were so close to him that we could see him even in the middle of the clouds. Our first burst hit the rear of the fuselage and knocked pieces off. The Yak pilot racked it over in a steep turn to the right and we gave him another burst along the right wing. This set the gas tank on fire and took the right flap and aileron off. By this time we were so close we almost collided with him.

'I could clearly see the pilot turn around and say something to the observer. Then, he pulled his canopy back and climbed out on the wing. Once again he leaned in and said something to the observer, but the latter was either scared or wounded as he never attempted to jump. The Yak pilot pulled the rip cord and the chute dragged him off the wing, just before the 'ship rolled over and went in.

'The action took place below 1000 ft. Later, we found that Moran had evaded his Yak and stalled out. When he recovered he found himself dead astern of the other Yak and shot it down.'

Maj Little, 339th commander, flying a racetrack pattern at higher altitude over Kimpo, saw the engagements below and heard 1st Lt Charles B Moran of Hudson's flight (in 46-357) say that he was being shot at. 'Poke' Little quickly led a pair of Twin Mustangs down into the fight.

As mentioned earlier, Moran pulled up abruptly out of his stall, recovering to shoot the second Yak down. Within minutes, Maj Little had also shot down another North Korean fighter, and two other 339th pilots claimed victories, but since no one could confirm them they were credited as probable kills. There is some evidence to suggest that Moran's kill may, in fact, have occurred minutes, or at least seconds, ahead of Hudson's, and that credit for being 'first' should not have gone to the latter.

The Twin Mustang seemed an unlikely candidate to be dominating Korean skies as it wasn't a jet, or even a well-known prop-driven aircraft. It had been created by joining two XP-51F fuselages (not P-51Hs, as widely reported) through a large centre wing section that housed the armament, plus a large parallel chord, single-piece, horizontal stabiliser. The fuselages were lengthened by 4 ft 9 in just aft of the radiator, and the area of the vertical fin was increased. The powerplant consisted of two liquid-cooled 2270 hp Allison V1710 piston engines, with opposite-rotating props to reduce torque – these gave the Twin Mustang a maximum speed of 460 mph at 21,000 ft. The version used in the Far East was the F-82G nightfighter, equipped with a SCR-720C search radar mounted between the paired fuselages. According to Lt Col Douglas E Smith of the 4th F(AW)S, 'Our particular aeroplanes sat in rows at the Downey, California, plant of North American from 1946 until 1948 while the Air Force tried to think up a useful role for them'. These gloss-black fighters were to continue in action with the 4th, 68th and 339th F(AW)Ss until mid-1951 when replaced by jets.

F-82G Twin Mustangs were painted in a gloss black finish for night

operations. Lettering, tail numbers and buzz numbers were painted in insignia red. Twin Mustangs of the 4th, 68th and 339th often wore unit emblems on their vertical fins and some had nicknames like *MID-NIGHT SINNER, OUR LI'L LASS* and "*DAQUAKE*". Diagonal stripes on the fuselages, and sometimes on drop tanks, denoted a squadron, group or wing commander's aircraft.

The F-82G was armed with six .50-calibre Colt-Browning M3 machine-guns mounted in the centre wing section, and firing exactly between the propeller arcs of the two engines. The aircraft carried 400 rounds per gun, 'which was a lot of ammunition', in the words of 1st Lt Ranald Adams, adjutant of the 68th F(AW)S.

The third day of the Korean War, and the first of aerial combat, was still unfolding when the 8th FBW's 35th Fighter Squadron (FS), nick-named the 'Panthers', flying F-80s out of Itazuke, became the first American jet squadron to down an enemy aircraft – the 8th FBW had three units, the 35th, with blue aircraft trim; the unnamed 36th, in red; and the 80th 'Headhunters', with yellow. The wing was also responsible for the F-82 force. Capt Raymond E Schillereff led four F-80s into the Seoul area and caught a quartet of Il-10s interfering with US transports loading at Seoul's Kimpo airfield – all four Ilyushins were shot down. Capt Schillereff and Lt Robert H Dewald each chalked up a kill, whilst Lt Robert E Wayne was credited with downing the remaining two Il-10s. The attackers succeeded, however, in destroying seven Republic of Korea

Line up shot of the 68th F(AW)S at Misawa air base, Japan, during the hectic summer of 1950. At far right is 46-383, alias *BUCKET O' BOLTS*, which claimed the first kill of the war just a matter of weeks after this shot was taken. Note how most of the Twin Mustangs wear nicknames on their noses *(George Deans)*

Maj James W 'Poke' Little was CO of the 339th F(AW)S, equipped with F-82Gs, and he added to his World War 2 score of seven victories by shooting down a La-7 on 27 June 1950. By the spring of 1951, he had moved on to command the 68th F(AW)S at Itazuke, where he posed for this shot with the enlisted men of his new unit. Only the three individuals in the centre foreground, namely the unit's first sergeant, Little and adjutant, 1st Lt Ranald Adams, are wearing the shade 84 blue uniform associated with the newly independent USAF. All the others wear khaki 'Ike' jackets and brown-brim wheel hats inherited from the Army *(via Randall Adams)*

When the Korean War began, the F-80C Shooting Star was the principal US fighter in the Far East. Pilots found it to be the best machine in the inventory for strafing, but the jet was rarely able to outmanoeuvre North Korea's propeller-driven Yakovlevs and Lavochkins, nor were the American jets initially equipped to carry bombs or rockets for air-to-ground duties. These Shooting Stars belong to the 8th FBW, the first USAF jet unit to see combat and shoot down an enemy aircraft. These feats took place within the first week of the conflict starting, the wing flying missions from the safety of its Itazuke base in Japan. However, by the time this shot was Taken in early 1951, the wing had moved much closer to the action, operating from the austere Suwon (K-13) site – these jets belong to the 80th FBS 'Headhunters' *(W G Sieber)*

Air Force (RoKAF) aircraft – T-6 Texans on the ground at Seoul City Airport.

The F-80 Shooting Star had been designed in 1943 and was America's first operational jet fighter. The F-80Cs employed in Korea were powered initially by a 4600 lb thrust Allison J33-A-23 turbojet engine, whilst late production C-models received 5400 lb thrust J33-A-35s. The F-80C was armed with six .50 cal machine-guns, with 300 rounds per weapon, in the nose. Assigned to the Orient purely as interceptors, the FEAF's F-80Cs initially lacked underwing shackles to carry bombs, although they were soon modified to fit (typically) two wingtip fuel tanks, a pair of 1000 lb bombs and eight underwing rockets. There was a price to be paid with this configuration, however. Due to centre-of-gravity problems, an F-80C loaded for an air-to-ground sortie could not carry the full load of 1800 rounds for its guns. The F-80C saw service with the 8th, 49th and 51st FWs in Korea.

Despite the success of Capt Schillereff and other F-80 pilots in jet-versus-prop air battles, no one was yet convinced that the Shooting Star was the right aircraft to deal with the North Korean Air Force. Some pilots felt that jets like the F-80 used up too much fuel and were, ironically, too *fast* to dogfight with the Yaks and Lavochkins. An article published by the Associated Press noted that it would take an F-80 as much as 40 miles to pull out of a high-speed pass (obviously an exaggeration), and that the Yaks could easily manoeuvre inside the turning radius of the US jet.

The 8th FBW attempted to overcome these problems by using its F-80s in a rather novel way. Fully loaded with .50 cal ammunition, but carrying none of the usual bombs or rockets, the F-80s flew to the Han River, near Seoul, and set up patrol orbits at 10,000 ft. They remained on station for 15 to 20 minutes, and if enemy aircraft appeared they engaged them. If not, the F-80s swooped over Seoul and made one or two passes against hostile road traffic, before returning to Itazuke.

By the morning of 28 June 1950, the North Korean army had broken through the resistance around Seoul and was storming the city. Truman gave MacArthur authority to evacuate only Americans. At first, air operations were restricted to South Korean airspace, and from bases in Japan and Guam, B-26s, B-29s, F-80s and F-82s opposed the assault.

MORE F-80 KILLS

On 29 June 1950 North Korean pilots bombed and strafed Suwon Most of these attacks were thwarted by fighter patrols, and during the morning F-80C pilots Lts William T Norris and Roy W Marsh shot down an La-7 and an Il-10. Later that day a bombing strike hit and completely destroyed a C-54 transport at the same airfield. The main terminal building at Kimpo was also riddled with holes from the bombing and strafing.

The F-51 also made its debut on 29 June, 1st Lt Richard J Burns shooting down an Il-10 and Lt Orrin R Fox going one better by claiming a pair.

Later in the day F-51 pilot Lt Harry T Sandlin shot down a La-7.

On 30 June, F-80s from Itazuke again tangled with North Korean fighters, Lts Charles A Wurster and John B Thomas (both from the 36th FBS/8th FBW) each shooting down a Yak-9. By now, the North Koreans had seized virtually all of Seoul, forcing Ambassador Muccio and his staff to abandon the embassy and flee from Suwon, which was to be overrun within days.

At this juncture, a Washington decision gave MacArthur free reign to employ US air power throughout the Korean peninsula 'against air bases, depots, tank farms, troop columns and other purely military targets such as bridges'. Within 24 hours, MacArthur also had authority to commit US ground troops, the 24th Infantry Division under Maj Gen William F Dean moving from Japan to Pusan. The United Nations security council, still able to act despite a Soviet boycott, passed a resolution supporting the defence of South Korea. Sixteen nations were to supply troops to fight the communists, whilst the USA, Australia and Britain would supply combat aircraft. South Africa also committed a fighter squadron, using borrowed American F-51s, whilst Canada rotated pilots through USAF units on exchange duty.

PASSION FIT was one of a handful of semi-retired F-51Ds given a brief reprieve from the scrap heap at Itazuke and issued back to its former unit within the partly F-80-transitioned 8th FBW. This machine wears the yellow fin strip of the 80th FBS, and was the personal mount of Lt Don Robertson. One of Robertson's squadron mates at the time was Lt Orrin R Fox, who shot down a pair of Il-10s on 29 June 1950 *(Don Robertson)*

On 30 June 1950, the Iwakuni, Japan-based, F-51Ds of the Royal Australian Air Force's (RAAF) No 77 Sqn were ordered to join the defence of South Korea. A week later, the unit suffered its first combat loss (on 7 July) when Sqn Ldr G Strout's Mustang (A68-757) was hit by ground fire and failed to return from a mission along the coast of North Korea.

Meanwhile, under MacArthur, Stratemeyer and Partridge, an allied air arm took shape to respond to the continuing North Korean advance, including the North Korean air threat. The Yakovlev, Lavochkin and Ilyushin pilots swarming over South Korea had learned to fly under Soviet tutelage, and many were veterans of World War 2 combat that had seen them serving within the Japanese imperial forces. The North Koreans did not pay attention to the concept of an 'ace', and did not regard an aerial victory as more important, or more praiseworthy, than air-to-ground bombing.

On 3 July 1950, eight F9F-3 Panthers of VF-51 'Screaming Eagles' launched from the wooden deck of *Valley Forge* to escort a strike on Pyongyang airfield. It was the first combat sortie ever by jet-propelled US Navy aircraft, and in the melee over Pyongyang, Ens E W Brown and Lt(jg) Leonard Plog each shot down a Yak-9. Two other VF-51 pilots destroyed Yaks on the ground.

The Navy was slower than the Air Force in adopting swept-wing fighters, and never had one in Korea – the straight-winged Panther remained the standard 'nautical' fighter throughout the war. The Navy/Marine

The second 8th FBW F-80 unit to find itself back on Mustangs was the 35th FBS 'Panthers', who marked their all-silver aircraft with blue trim. 1st Lt Richard J Burns scored the squadron's first aerial kill on the same day as Orrin Fox when he also 'bagged' an Il-10. These smiling groundcrew were photographed at Kimpo soon after the Pusan breakout *(James Tidwell)*

When the Korean War began on 25 June 1950, the USS *Valley Forge* (CVA-45) was cruising near Hong Kong with a carrier air group of combat aircraft, whilst a second carrier, USS *Philippine Sea* (CVA-47), was en route. 'Happy Valley's' air group included VF-51 and -52 with F9F-3 Panthers and VF-53 and -54 with F4U-4B Corsairs. On 3 July 1950, Panther pilots Ens E W Brown and Lt(jg) Leonard Plog of VF-51 each shot down a Yak-9 *(Douglas)*

This F9F-2B (BuNo 123713) belongs to VF-721, an activated reserve squadron operating from USS *Kearsage* (CVA-33) on the carrier's only Korean combat cruise between 11 August 1952 and 17 March 1953

Corps operated the F9F-2 with the 5000 lb thrust Pratt & Whitney J42-P-6 (license-built Nene), F9F-3 with the 4600 lb thrust Allison J33-A-8 and F9F-5 with the 6250 lb thrust Pratt & Whitney J48-P-6A (license-built Tay) turbojet engine. Aircraft with six wing pylons were initially designated F9F-2B, whilst all Panthers were armed with four 20 mm cannon.

Suwon duly fell. C-54 Skymasters brought in the first American ground troops to face North Korea's T-34 tanks, but they were ill-prepared, ill-equipped and quickly overrun. The tanks kept coming.

If the Shooting Star was too fast for air-to-air combat with Yaks, it was also too fast for the air-to-ground support duties now foisted upon it. 'The F-80 was an extremely stable platform for gunnery and bombing', remembers one 8th FBW pilot from the early days of the war, 'but we also knew that we couldn't "jink" or take evasive action if we wanted to have much prospect of hitting the enemy'. Pilots who'd triumphed in aerial engagements were frustrated by their air-to-ground role as the war went from bad to worse.

In the only aerial victory on 17 July 1950, and the first in 17 days, F-80C pilot Capt Francis B Clark (35th FBS/8th FBW) shot down a Yak-9. Two days later a trio of kills were chalked up. F-80C pilots 2nd Lt Elwood A Kees and 1st Lts Robert D McKee and Charles W Wurster (36th FBS/8th FBW) each flamed a Yak-9. Along with Robert E Wayne, Wurster became the second American – and one of just three in 1950 – to achieve two aerial victories.

On 20 July 1950, Taejon fell to the North Koreans. Only the Naktong River at Taegu – the northern demarcation of what soldiers called the Pusan Perimeter – lay between the invaders and the sea. That day, F-80 pilots 2nd Lt David H Goodnough and Capt Robert L Lee (35th FBS/8th FBW) each shot down a Yak-9. Although the Korean War was now in a critical period, there was not to be another air-to-air kill for 103 days (until November 1).

On the ground, the war was going poorly for the UN allies, but at least the North Koreans still had no jet aircraft and failed to provide any air support for their troops. With 20 aerial victories in the first month of the conflict, the Allies

could legitimately claim to have swept the North Korean air arm from the skies over the peninsula.

Warplanes from the British carrier HMS *Triumph* were now part of the fight in Korea, although they did not immediately see air-to-air action. RAF pilots also served exchange tours with American units, as well as being assigned to the RAAF's No 77 Sqn. By 22 July 1950, US Navy pilots were carrying out especially difficult close air support missions in the Pusan pocket.

On 1 August 1950, *Philippine Sea* arrived off the coast of Korea, joined by the escort carriers USS *Badoeng Strait* (CVE-116) and *Sicily* (CVE-118). Aboard CVA-47 was Carrier Air Group 11, with VF-111 and -112 (F9F-2 Panther), VF-113 and -114 (F4U-4 Corsair) and VA-115 (AD-4Q Skyraider) aboard. *Badoeng Strait* carried Marine Corps squadron VMF-323 'Death Rattlers', flying F4U-4 and F4U-4B Corsairs. *Sicily*, with World War 2 ace Capt James S Thach at the helm, came into the war with VMF-214 'Blacksheep' embarked, the unit being equipped with F4U-4B Corsairs. Soon, Marine F4U-5Ns of VMF(N)-513 'Flying Nightmares', a nightfighter unit commanded by Maj J Hunter Reinburg, began operating from Itazuke. The missions flown by these squadrons set a pattern of operations for others to follow over the next three years.

On 5 August 1950, Maj Louis J Sebille, commander of the newly-arrived 67th FBS/18th FBW, led a flight of Mustangs against North Korean artillery and troop positions dug in along a riverbank near Hamchang, flying F-51D 44-74394. Sebille hit his target, banked, circled, and radioed in his wingmen to make a strafing pass.

Ground fire sent shells whipping around the Mustangs. Sebille's aircraft was hit, and he called in his wingman to survey the damage. The latter thought it was serious and urged him to return to Taegu. Instead, Sebille again rolled in on the target and opened fire with his

This formation shot was taken just after the first anniversary of the FEAF's involvement in Korea, four of the main combatant types being put up for a one-off fly-by. Leading the quartet is a soon to be retired F-82G of the 68th F(AW)S, with its replacement, the F-94B, sitting off its right wing. To the Twin Mustang's left is a 35th FIW F-80C, whilst in the trail slot is an F-86A of the 4th FIW – all four types enjoyed varying degrees of success against communist aircraft *(via Jerry Scutts)*

This F-51D exhibits the markings of the 67th FBS, based at Chinhae (K-10) in August 1950. Beneath its wings are six High Velocity Aerial Rockets (HVARs), the staple weapon of most attack units throughout the war. The squadron was lead into battle by Maj Louis J Sebille, who was posthumously awarded a Medal of Honor just days after arriving in-theatre when he flew his damaged F-51 into enemy troop emplacements dug into a riverbank near Hamchung *(Tom Shockley)*

A SAAF F-51D of No 2 Sqn taxies away from its hardstanding to begin yet another ground-attack sortie in 1951. The unit's distinctive 'Flying Cheetah' emblem is visible below the cockpit, whilst the pennant worn above the motif, plus the multi-coloured prop-boss, denote that this machine belongs to the Officer Commanding No 2 Sqn

VMA-312 'Checkerboards' were one of two F4U-4-equipped units dispatched into a crater strewn Kimpo airfield days after it had been recaptured by UN forces. Once established, the squadron went to work providing round-the-clock support for ground forces pushing the communists back into North Korea. VMA-312 continued to follow UN troops north during their rapid advance, soon moving to the liberated strip at Wonsan

six machine-guns. Hit many times on this final pass, he flew straight into the concentration of enemy troops, where his F-51 exploded in their midst. For sacrificing his life, Maj Louis J Sebille posthumously became the first flier in Korea to be awarded the Medal of Honor.

SOUTH AFRICANS

South Africa's role in Korea got under way on 5 September 1950 when No 2 'Flying Cheetahs' Sqn formed under World War 2 ace, Commandant S van Breda Theron. The unit was to operate as part of the USAF's 18th FBW for the entire war, suffering terrible losses on low-level bombing and strafing missions – ironically, they never scored a single aerial victory during the conflict.

While the Allies were being thrown back, Gen MacArthur plotted Operation *Chromite* – the amphibious landing behind the lines at Inchon, west of Seoul. The invasion took place on 15-16 September 1950, the Marines quickly recapturing Kimpo airport and, soon afterward, Seoul. The North Koreans were thrown into confusion, their army, successful in the first weeks of the conflict, now beginning to fold and retreat. VMF(N)-542 'Flying Tigers' arrived at Kimpo on 19 September 1950 and soon had 24 twin-engine, two-seat, F7F-3N Tigercats in place. Also arriving at Kimpo were VMF-212 'Lancers' and VMA-312 'Checkerboards' (both with F4U-4 Corsairs). The USAF, too, began to move into the Seoul region's principal airfield.

Korean waters were breached on 8 October 1950 by USS *Leyte* (CVA-32) with fighter squadrons VF-31 (F9F-2 Panthers), -32 and -33 (F4U-4 Corsairs), as well as VA-35 (AD-3 Skyraiders). HMS *Theseus* replaced *Triumph* off the Korean coast, enabling the Royal Navy to introduce the Hawker Sea Fury, which equipped No 807 Sqn.

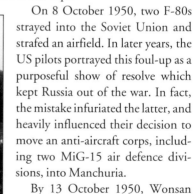

On 8 October 1950, two F-80s strayed into the Soviet Union and strafed an airfield. In later years, the US pilots portrayed this foul-up as a purposeful show of resolve which kept Russia out of the war. In fact, the mistake infuriated the latter, and heavily influenced their decision to move an anti-aircraft corps, including two MiG-15 air defence divisions, into Manchuria.

By 13 October 1950, Wonsan was in UN hands, and USMC Tigercats and Corsairs began flying combat missions from the recaptured airfield soon after. Pyongyang fell a week later.

ENTER THE MiG

On 1 November 1950, six swept-wing jet fighters attacked F-51D Mustangs. The jets came from across the Yalu River – the border to China which Allied pilots were forbidden to cross. At first, little attention was devoted to these MiG-15s, with 1 November also being notable as the day that F-51D pilots Capts Alma R Flake and Robert D Thresher of the 67th FBS/18th FBW each shot down a North Korean prop-driven fighter, listed on the official record as Yak-3s.

Flake then destroyed a Yak-9 the following day to join F-80 'jocks' Robert E Wayne and Charles W Wurster in reaching a total score of two kills. That same day, another Yak-9 was flamed by 1st Lt James L Glessner, Jr, of the 12th FBS/18th FBW whilst flying another Mustang – his sharkmouthed 45-11736 was just four away from being the final P-51D manufactured. On 6 November Capt Howard I Price, yet another 67th FBS flier, was given credit for 1.5 Yak-9 kills, the half-share being split with with 1st Lt Henry S Reynolds.

No one in the West – not in G-2 (intelligence) or in Gen Mac-Arthur's command post in Tokyo – knew much about the swept-wing jet fighters reported by Mustang pilots on 1 November. Instead, the Americans were busily planning for the war to end before the coming Christmas holidays! Lt Col Clure Smith, an F-80C pilot with 1.5 kills from World War 2 who now com-

manded the 25th FIS/51st FIW, returned from a sortie with a gun-camera photo of a MiG-15. No one seemed to think it mattered *what* the Chinese were flying as the enemy, after all, was North Korea.

This premise was totally wrong. The MiG-15s were being flown on combat patrols by Russians, and on the rare occasion when the Allies monitored the Russian language in VHF radio transmissions, the assumption was made that Soviet advisors were helping out with pilot conversion. In fact, at this stage of the conflict red-nosed Russian MiG-15s were being both flown and maintained by Russians at all times.

An enigma in the West at the time of its debut over Korea, the MiG-15 was named after the Soviet Union's Mikoyan-Gurevich design bureau and was a mid-wing monoplane incorporating 35 degrees of wing sweep, its flight surface based in part on the same German swept-wing research which contributed to the Sabre. The maiden flight of the MiG (on 30 December 1947) came just 90 days after the Sabre's, the jet being initially powered by the 4500 lb thrust RD-45F turbojet inspired by the British Nene – examples of this revolutionary engine had been sold to the USSR soon after the war. The MiG-15 was armed with one 37 mm NS-37 and two 23 mm NS- or NR-23 (the NR being faster firing) cannons, and it boasted a maximum speed of 640 mph at 10,000 ft.

The MiG-15 made its first appearance in-theatre when four of the Soviet-built jets attacked F-51s over North Korea in November 1950. Armed with one 37 and two 23 mm cannon, and able to begin an air-to-air engagement at higher altitude than any Allied fighter (including the F-86), the MiG-15 was a formidable opponent. The first MiGs to enter combat were flown by pilots of the Soviet air forces, who rotated entire fighter regiments through Manchuria. Later, Chinese pilots manned the bulk of the MiG-15 force. The example shown here wears standard North Korean markings (a red star in a red circle, surrounded by a blue circle) although 'native' pilots only began flying the MiG-15 very late on in the 1950-53 conflict *(William H Myers)*

On 8 November 1950, 1st Lt Russell J Brown was flying an F-80C Shooting Star (49-0713, *ELENE*) normally assigned to 1st Lt Jack Smith of the 16th FIS/51st FIW (Brown belonged to the 26th FIS) on a mission from Kimpo. He and his wingmen turned aggressively into half a dozen MiG-15s, splitting up the formation and sending five scurrying back across the Yalu towards Antung. The sixth MiG broke in the wrong direction and appeared below Brown's F-80.

'Damn', Brown said out loud, 'I'm going to get him'. He pushed over and dived behind the MiG-15. Though all but one of his guns was jammed, Brown unleashed bursts of .50 calibre gunfire which struck the

fighter, set it afire, and sent it spinning in engulfed in flames. This was history's first jet-versus-jet aerial victory.

On 9 November 1950, MiG-15s shot up an RB-29 and forced it to crash-land, killing five crewmen. However, a gunner aboard the Superfortress, Staff Sergeant Harry J Lavene of the 91st Reconnaissance Squadron, did manage to shoot down one of the MiGs. The following day, MiG-15s downed another B-29 near the Yalu.

On 10 November 1950, Lt Cdr William Thomas Amen, pilot of a Navy F9F-2 Panther, shot down a MiG-15 – the commander of VF-111 (aboard *Philippine Sea*) bagged his kill at low altitude. Later in the day, two *Valley Forge* pilots shared a second MiG, also at low altitude, whilst a third Navy MiG kill came a week later. Still, the UN Allies failed to grasp the significance of the jets, and the role of the Russians.

In a stunning move, China inserted half a million troops into North Korea. Beginning on 26 November 1950, hordes of Chinese soldiers attacked across the front. It happened overnight while Allied intelligence experts were 'asleep at the switch', and UN forces awoke to find their positions opposed by no fewer than 50 Chinese divisions.

About 400 Soviet-built MiG-15 fighters were now at the ready on the north side of the Yalu. The Allies had no fighter to cope with the MiG-15, and it seemed poised to wrestle air supremacy by clearing the skies of American B-26s and B-29s. But despite the MiG-15 being the world's best interceptor at that point in time, it lacked the ability to be a fighter-bomber. A lightweight fighter that was neither big or complex, it was never used in Korea for long-range missions and, indeed, was conspicuous by its absence over the front lines throughout the conflict.

Being a single-purpose fighter was no impediment to the MiG-15 if it wanted to command the air-to-air arena. There was nothing to prevent it from controlling the skies up north, neutralising the Allies' bombing campaign by destroying aircraft like the B-26, B-29, F-80 and F-84 virtually at will.

On the same day that MiG-15s made their first appearance over Korea, the humble F-51 was adding more kills to its already impressive score – two Yak-3s were shot down by the 67th FBS, the operators of this battle-weary Mustang seen at Chinhae *(Max Tomich)*

Shortly after downing a MiG-15 on 8 November 1950 in history's first jet-v-jet engagement, 1st Lt Russell Brown poses in the cockpit of F-80C 49-737. However, on his MiG-killing mission Brown was flying 48-713, which had Jack Smith's name on the canopy rails. The former belonged to the 26th FIS, but he was flying with the 16th – both were part of the 51st FIW *(USAF)*

SABRE DEBUT

On the day of Lt Brown's F-80 kill, the USAF ordered the 4th Fighter Interceptor Wing (FIW) at Wilmington County, Delaware, to pack up and move with its F-86A Sabres. Until then, the swept-wing jet had been the sole property of the Air Defense Command, which guarded North America against possible attack from the Soviet Union.

The F-86 was the first American fighter to exploit German swept-wing research. Conceived as a day fighter, the A-model was powered initially by a 4850 lb thrust General Electric J47-GE-1 axial-flow turbojet engine, and was capable of a maximum speed of 707 mph at sea level. The first Sabre (XP-86) may have flown faster than sound *before* the first 'official' supersonic flight (on 14 October 1947) by Chuck Yeager's Bell XS-1 rocket aeroplane. Armament was six .50 cals. Over time, an improved Sabre was to become the world's premier fighter, but early F-86As, including those of the 4th FIW had technical problems galore.

The 4th, commanded by Col George F Smith, boasted some of the best jet fighter pilots in the USAF, most of them World War 2 veterans. The wing's 4th Fighter Interceptor Group (FIG) was headed by Col John C Meyer, the Eighth Air Force's second ranking ace of World War 2. Its squadrons were the 334th 'Pidgeons' (later renamed the 'Eagles'), 335th 'Chiefs' and 336th FIS 'Rocketeers'. F-86As of the 4th FIW were wrapped in protective cocoons and craned aboard the escort carrier USS *Cape Esperance* (CVE-88), which duly arrived at Yokosuka, Japan, on 1 December 1950.

Later that same month the Chinese air force's MiG-15s – Soviet air forces jets in reality – began to press home the fight. Most Allied warplanes were useless against the Soviet fighter, although some MiGs took hits from UN aircraft nonetheless. For example, on 12 December 1950, F-80C pilot 1st Lt Evan Rosencrans was credited with damaging a MiG.

He recalls that, 'It was early afternoon and four of us in F-80s were flying top cover for Shooting Stars attacking the Sinuiju airfield on the Korean side of the Yalu. It was a beautifully clear day and while we were doing our best to avoid the anti-aircraft fire from the Chinese side, we saw the MiGs launch from Antung. In a very short time the anti-aircraft fire stopped and there were 12 MiGs at about 2000 to 3000 ft below us, four off the left wing, four off the right and four behind us.

'I was the flight leader and began edging to the right to try to get under that flight of four, thus reducing the odds. We were flying roughly in a north-westerly direction at that time. Just then the four off our left wing attacked. We dropped our wing tanks and broke left. As soon as the number four MiG passed, the four off our right wing attacked and we broke right. I should add that all three flights of MiGs attacked "in string" – one after another, in each flight. Again, as soon as the number four man passed, the four that were originally behind us attacked. I fired and hit the number four man in that flight all the way from his air intake to the tailpipe. The surviving MiGs went back to Antung.'

F-80C pilots racked up half a dozen MiG kills, but the straight-wing Shooting Star with its centrifugal-flow jet engine was quickly relegated to air-to-ground work. These jets wear the blue nose paintwork and red fuselage and tail strips of the 16th FIS/51st FIW – 1st Lt Brown scored his historic MiG victory in a jet from this unit

On 10 November 1950 Lt Cdr William Thomas Amen, pilot of a US Navy F9F-2 Panther, shot down a MiG-15 at low altitude, then posed for this portrait the following day. Amen was commander of VF-111 'Sundowners', part of Air Group 11 aboard *Philippine Sea*, at the time. Later in the day, two *Valley Forge* pilots shared a second MiG kill, also at low altitude. A third Navy MiG kill was to come within a week. On the canopy rails of Amen's Panther are the names of his plane captain and armourer. The jet's four 20 mm cannon had a higher rate of fire than those fitted to the MiG-15, and proved deadly in combat (*US Navy*)

No F-80 could hold the line forever, and on 13 December 1950, Lt Col Meyer moved an advance detachment of 4th FIW F-86A Sabres from Johnson to Kimpo. C-54 Skymasters brought in support personnel, who arrived to find the site virtually untenable. The base was not equipped to handle F-86As, whose number, over a fortnight, grew to 32, whilst the knowledge of an oncoming Chinese advance did little to help morale. Finally, exceedingly bad winter weather made it necessary for pilots to delay their first Sabre flights for some days.

Snow and low scudding clouds finally 'broke' north of snow-covered Kimpo on 17 December 1950, allowing the hulking six-foot two-inch Lt Col Bruce Hinton, commander of the 336th FIS 'Rocketeers', and pilot of an F-86A-5 (49-1236 *Squanee*), to lead 'Baker Flight's' four Sabres on the wing's inaugural patrol over the Yalu. They were flying what was to become known as a fighter sweep – bait to get the communist MiGs airborne. The slab of land along the Yalu was soon nicknamed MiG Alley.

The 'Chinese' (actually Russians) apparently mistook Hinton's Sabres for slower F-80s. Warned by his wingman that MiGs were coming their way, Hinton turned his flight to engage four of the enemy jets. The MiGs crossed his flight path a mile ahead and Hinton ordered drop tanks to be jettisoned, only to find that his radio was malfunctioning. Confusion followed as Hinton dropped his tanks and accelerated ahead of his flight. He quickly turned behind an element of two MiGs, whose pilots apparently thought that they could simply outrun the fighter behind them. Hinton dived after the MiG flight leader and was able to get on his 'six o'clock' position. He fired a short burst and saw what looked like debris falling away from the MiG – the jet was also streaming fluid, possibly fuel.

Hinton then took on the number two MiG and found himself bucking in his jet wash. He adjusted his position and fired a long burst which hit the MiG's engine. Hinton stayed in a left turn behind his opponent and had a spectacular view of the Russian fighter. He closed in and fired again, keeping his trigger depressed. The rear section of the MiG was consumed by flames and the jet rolled on its back and went plummeting to earth. It crashed 10 miles southeast of the Yalu, and there was no parachute. Bruce Hinton had just scored the first aerial victory to be credited to the F-86.

This kill had not been achieved easily though, Hinton having nearly exhausted his Sabre's full load of 1802 rounds. He'd fought aggressively and he'd shown that American pilots, generally, were more skilled than their Chinese adversaries. But Hinton had also shown that the MiG-15 was damnably difficult to bring down out of the sky.

On 19 December 1950, Lt Col Glenn T Eagleston, 334th FIS boss and Sabre pilot, damaged a MiG-15. It was a modest start that added to Eagleston's 18.5 kills previously scored with the 353rd FG in Europe during World War 2. On 22 December, MiGs bounced a flight of eight Sabres and shot down Capt Lawrence V Bach's F-86A, which took cannon hits in the wing roots and spun away in flames – their first Sabre kill was made possible simply because the MiG could fly higher than the F-86A.

Also on 22 December, Navy exchange pilot Lt Cdr Paul E Pugh led a four-jet flight in company with four other Sabres. Pugh heard MiGs called while cruising 20 miles south of the Yalu at 32,000 ft. He turned his flight into the threat, only to see a MiG-15 pass close aboard – too

1st Lt Evan W Rosencrans achieved the difficult feat of damaging a MiG-15 while flying an F-80C on 12 December 1950 over Sinuiju. The meeting between the swept-wing communist fighter and the straight-wing American jets was reported by US pilots as 'a new type of air warfare used by the communists', as the MiGs attacked together in one flight instead of coming in singly *(USAF)*

close in fact to shoot. The two fighters passed canopy-to-canopy and Pugh racked his Sabre into a hard reversal, picking up the bandit diving for the undercast. Pugh later said, 'I cut across his turn and fired. I hit him pretty good. Then he disappeared into the cloud deck'.

In pursuit, Pugh broke into the clear and found the MiG flying straight and level at about 500 ft. 'I just "drove" up behind him', Paul recounted, 'and got the MiG kill'. That same day Lt Col Eagleston was also credited with destroying a MiG-15. His kill was scored during an eight-Sabre prolonged fray with 15 MiGs in a twisting, close-quarters, dogfight. MiG-15 victories were also credited to Col John C Meyer (adding to his 24 kills with the 352nd FG in World War 2), 1st Lt Arthur L O'Connor and Capts John Odinorne and James O Roberts.

On 30 December 1950, Lt Cdr Pugh became the first F-86 pilot to rack up a second MiG kill, whilst Capt James Jabara opened his account with a probable. The Sabre-equipped 4th FIW could now claim eight kills and two probables against just one air-to-air loss (although Pugh's second victory, inexplicably ignored by the USAF, never became part of its records). These eight kills were to remain the total score for 1950, and were to be the final such victories for more than three months.

SABRE VERSUS MiG

4th FIW pilots had by this stage learned that early F-86As had at least as many mechanical problems as any other new aircraft. Pilots particularly encountered problems with unreliable gun chargers, but worse still, their opponents always looked down at the Sabres from a higher altitude with impunity. If they chose to remain at maximum height, no F-86 could get near them. The MiGs controlled the time and place of every fight.

The comparison between the F-86 and the MiG-15 was to be made again and again by men on both sides. The latter was able to fly higher, thus offering a decisive advantage at the start of a battle. Early Sabre models were inferior in other respects, too, and a Soviet perspective on the comparison between the F-86 and the MiG is offered by Korean veteran, Maj Gen Georgy Lobov.

'The MiG-15 in its main characteristics surpassed all similar enemy aircraft except the F-86. In comparison with the latter, the MiG had a better rate of climb and thrust-to-weight ratio, but was somewhat inferior in manoeuvrability and radius of action. Their maximum flight speeds, however, were roughly equal. The F-86 had a better fuselage aerodynamic form. This fighter gained speed in a dive faster than ours and had a lesser 'sink' rate than the MiG-15 when recovering from a dive.

'The MiG-15 armament was more powerful and consisted of two 23 and one 37 mm (cannon) in a good arrangement. The American fighters and fighter-bombers had up to six 12.7 mm (.50 calibre) Colt-Browning machine-guns scattered along the wing'. In fact, while prop-driven US fighters had wing guns, jet fighters had guns in the nose. A notable advantage of the F-86 was its better sighting equipment, especially the radar rangefinder which automatically made corrections for range. On the MiG-15, range to target was determined visually and the data input by hand into a semi-automatic sight.'

Facing a superior number of MiGs, 4th FIW commander, Col George F Smith, became the first of many (quickly joined by group commander

The first man to open the Sabre's MiG killing account in Korea was Lt Col Bruce Hinton, and he did so on 17 December 1950 in this very F-86A-5 (49-1236), nicknamed *Squanee*. Commander of the 4th FIG's 336th FIS, Hinton was leading the group's very first combat patrol over the Yalu when he achieved this historic kill, the attacking quartet of MiGs apparently mistaking the Sabre four-ship for Shooting Stars. This shot was taken some five months after Hinton's victory (*Malcolm Norton*)

Already trailing smoke, a mortally damaged MiG-15 loses height as its pilot makes a last ditch bid for safety northwards over the Yalu River, which is clearly visible in the distance. Damage inflicted by the pursuing Sabre can be seen just outboard of the fuselage/wing root join – this jet was one of eight MiGs destroyed by the 4th FIG in December 1950 *(via Jerry Scutts)*

Lt Col Meyer) to complain to Fifth Air Force HQ that his Sabre force was hamstrung with intolerable supply and maintenance problems. Though working conditions at Kimpo were not as bad as anticipated, despite the snow and cold, there was almost nothing to work with. Small, simple, parts needed to keep the jets in the air were almost impossible to obtain, and while the Chinese swarmed down the pike, support problems kept Sabres grounded, eroding morale, and giving the MiG pilots the upper hand.

The 4th FIW's newly-arrived Sabres were destined to reside at Kimpo for a mere three weeks before being kicked out by the Chinese. Meyer, Hinton, Frey and others struggled to defeat weather, maintenance problems and flagging morale to get into action against the MiGs. New Year's Eve was filled with the frenetic activity of men preparing to evacuate. As 1951 began, 500,000 Chinese poured southward. MiG-15s, nominally belonging to Chinese air divisions but really piloted by Russians, dominated MiG Alley along the Yalu River, but stayed north of the battlefield. With the Chinese approaching, chaos reigned at Kimpo airfield. Equipment was dismantled and convoys moved out. The 4th FIG (F-86A), 51st FIG (F-80C) and 67th TRS (RF-51D) were being withdrawn.

The 4th consisted of 32 aeroplanes and a composite group of pilots headed by Col Meyer, who ordered that some Sabres had to be flown out before the New Year began. On 1 January a distracted airman was sucked into the engine air intake of an F-86A and killed, a mishap perhaps compounded by the urgency of the Chinese onslaught, and proof that working around jets was a serious business. The Sabre's presence in Korea ended the next day. Capt Howard M Lane flew out the aircraft which had taken the airman's life and now lacked an air speed indicator. On his wing, Capt Max Weill flew the 32nd, and last, Sabre.

Other members of the 4th FIW, including MiG-killer, Lt Col Bruce Hinton, were left behind with no Sabres. They got out of Kimpo on the night of 2 January in a C-54 as the airfield came under attack from small-arms fire – it was almost completely surrounded by the Chinese. The enemy were coming through the wire as the transport lifted off, and they overran the South Korean capital in the early hours of 4 January 1951.

CHINESE ASSAULT

As 1951 unfolded, UN forces were to halt their withdrawal, launch a counter-attack, and recapture Seoul. But they were to go no farther. The battle lines on the ground hardly changed in the months and years ahead.

Beginning 14 January 1951, an F-86A detachment of the 4th FIW returned to Korea to begin flying air-to-ground missions from Taegu, far in the south – 158 sorties were flown in this first attempt to use the Sabre as a fighter-bomber. 21 January 1951 brought a momentary change in fortune for the FEAF. Lt Col William E Bertram was up near the Yalu in one of the first F-84Es brought to Korea by the 27th Fighter-Escort Wing (FEW). In a glancing engagement with MiG-15s from the other side of the river, Thunderjet pilot Bertram managed to get solid hits with .50 calibre bursts, duly shooting the MiG out of the sky.

On 23 January, while B-29s were attacking Pyongyang, Col Ashley B Packard, commander of the 27th FEW, persuaded higher-ups to 'frag' (assign) his F-84Es to hit the airfield at Sinuiju, just south of the Yalu. Thirty-three Thunderjets took off from the pierced-steel runway at Taegu, flew north, and hit the airfield by surprise. The first eight, assigned a strafing role, began working the place over, but once the rest of Packard's force had descended over Sinuiju, MiGs scrambled from Antung. A battle ensued, and four of the latter were shot down by Lt Jacob Kratt (two kills) and Capts Allen McGuire and William W Slaughter. For reasons which are unclear, McGuire's kill does not appear on official records – all Thunderjets returned home safely.

The F-84 was the USAF's final jet fighter to have straight wings, and was severely underpowered at first. Following its maiden flight (on 28 February 1946), it faced myriad problems resulting from ever-increasing structural weight and low engine thrust. The Korean War's F-84D version (which entered combat after the F-84E) was modestly powered by the 5000 lb thrust J35-A-17D, and the E- and G-models, also used in Korea, offered only small improvements in terms of thrust. The F-84 had been ordered by the USAF from Republic to insure against the failure of the Sabre, and pilots knew it.

The E-model had a lengthened fuselage (by 12-in) to improve cockpit accommodation, revised wingtip tanks and a radar gunsight. The G-model offered greater power with its 5600 lb thrust J35-A-29, but its primary mission was outside the scope of the Korean problem – it was the first single-seat fighter designed from the outset to carry atomic bombs. Korean F-84D, E- and G-model Thunderjets were armed with six .50 cals, with 300 rounds per gun, and could it haul up to 6000 lb of external bombs and rockets. The F-84G was credited with a maximum speed of 616 mph at 10,000 ft.

The F-84Es of Col Packard's 27th FEW flew 2076 combat sorties in January 1951, before moving from Taegu back to Itazuke. The Thunderjet had better range than the F-80, and the 27th FEW continued sorties from Japan against communist ground targets.

On 5 February 1951, Maj Arnold 'Moon' Mullins, pilot of an F-51D Mustang, and commander of the 67th FBS (one of three squadrons in the 18th FBW), was credited with shooting down a North Korean Yak-3 fighter. Although this was the third time that a Yak-3 had been credited to an American pilot, some observers believe that the piston-engined fighters were actually Yak-9s that had been identified incorrectly. To further confuse things, most of Mullins' squadron mates remember him being credited with *three* or *four* Yak kills, though the record only awards him one.

When a Yak-9 was test-flown at Wright Field, USAF experts learned a great deal about it, but Yak-Mustang encounters were too few and too fleet for an effective combat comparison of the best World War 2 fighters fielded by the two superpowers to be formulated.

The F-86 returned to the war in earnest when the 4th FIW moved back to Korea, this time to Suwon. Just before their arrival, a slashing attack by MiG-15s damaged no fewer than ten B-29s, three of which made emergency landings at Taegu. On that 1 March 1951 mission, Staff Sergeant William H Finnegan, a gunner aboard a Superfortress of the 343rd Bomb Squadron, was credited with a MiG-15 kill.

The reappearance of the Sabres blunted the MiG threat to the B-29 force. Air-to-air fighting persisted at a reduced level, and on 17 March Shooting Star pilot 1st Lt Howard J Landry of the 36th FBS/8th FBW joined the handful of F-80 jocks who had achieved the exceedingly difficult task of 'bagging' a MiG-15. Two gunners aboard B-29s, Staff Sergeant Norman S Greene and Technical Sergeant Charles W Summers, both members of the 28th BS, were credited with further MiG kills on 30 March. The following day, F-86 pilot Flt Lt Omer Levesque (a Royal Canadian Air Force exchange pilot) of the 334th FIS/4th FIW became the first RCAF pilot to shoot down a MiG.

That month, Gen Stratemeyer cabled USAF chief of staff Gen Hoyt S Vandenberg, describing his concern for the vulnerability of F-51s and F-80s to MiG attack. He requested that all Fifth Air Force fighter-bomber wings be re-equipped with F-84E Thunderjets. Vandenberg approved the request, but it was not to materialise until early 1953.

By now, the principal characteristics of the Sabre versus MiG confrontation were becoming clear. The MiG-15 enjoyed the important advantage of a much higher service ceiling. While a 'clean' F-86A could barely struggle along at 42,000 ft, the MiG-15 cruised at 50,000 ft or higher. Since the Sabres had to travel north from 200 miles south of MiG Alley, they had to spend most of their fuel commuting, and had little time to spend in combat. Unlike the MiGs, the Sabres had no GCI (ground control intercept) network to vector them onto an enemy, although the radar station on Cho-do island, callsign 'Dentist', was helpful some of the time. Most advantages seemed to rest with the communist side, however.

In one of the great ironies of the war, the first double-MiG kill was scored not by the ever-dominant F-86, but by its more humble second, the F-84. This feat was achieved on 23 January 1951 by Lt Jacob Kratt in an F-84E of the 522nd FES/27th FEG, his unit being tasked with 'fragging' Sinuiju as a diversionary strike whilst B-29s attacked Pyongyang. This 522nd jet was photographed by 'Jake' Kratt whilst returning from another escort mission 'up north' soon after his double strike

The Yak-9 was the most advanced fighter in the North Korean inventory when the fighting began on 25 June 1950, but by early 1951 had ceded its pure fighter role to 'Chinese' MiG-15s. Most were Yak-9P versions – *Pushyechnyi*, signifying cannon armament. The Yak-9 had sufficient range and staying power to give a good account of itself against Allied fighters, but North Korea started the war alone without direct help from its Soviet and Chinese allies, and its pilots lacked the experience to fight effectively against their adversaries. During the brief flurry of air combat in June and July 1950 – one of the few occasions when American fighters fought over friendly ground and their adversaries travelled some distance to reach the fray – 20 North Korean aircraft were shot down, most of them Yak-9s. This Yak-9P was captured after the Allies reversed the tide of war with the Inchon landing and overran communist airfields. Evaluated at Cornell Aero Lab and test-flown at Wright-Patterson AFB in 1951, the Yak was later displayed briefly at the Air Force Museum in the 1950s, but was sadly scrapped soon afterwards *(USAF)*

Capt James Jabara of the 334th FIS/4th FIW got his first confirmed MiG on 3 April 1951, with Lt Col Benjamin H Emmert (335th FIS) – a six-kill ace from the Mediterranean theatre in World War 2 – and 1st Lts Roy W McLain (334th FIS) and William B Yancey, Jr (336th FIS), bringing the day's tally to four. Jabara, who had been credited with 1.5 kills in Europe six years earlier, was soon to eclipse them in the jet war.

Although he'd never fired at an enemy aircraft before, one of the most respected fighter pilots in the USAF was Maj Edward C Fletcher, ops officer for the 4th Wing's 334th FS. In the years that followed the Korean War, a number of the aces shifted to air defence squadrons, and Fletcher eventually commanded many of them. He had that quality that cannot be defined – a blend of aggressiveness and sound leadership. But Fletcher only ever 'bagged' a single MiG-15, which he claimed on 4 April.

On 7 April, 48 F-84Es of the 27th FEW escorted B-29s to the railway bridge at Sinuiju. Thirty MiGs pounced, and although only one got through, it downed a B-29 belonging to the 307th BG. As for the target, the bridge was battered, but still standing. Two days later Sabre pilot 1st Lt Arthur L O'Connor (336th FIS) tallied up his second, and final, MiG kill. The next day, Jabara doubled his score.

On 12 April, three bomber groups hit the Sinuiju bridge again. MiGs swarmed down through Sabre screens and escorting Thunderjets, and at least two B-29s were shot down and five damaged. This furious fighting, marked by aggressive MiG attacks on B-29s, brought the USAF a total of 11 kills, including seven MiGs downed by Superfortress gunners (of ten claimed), plus three 'probables' by F-84s.

Jim Jabara destroyed his third MiG during this period, tying him with F-84 pilot Kratt as the top-scoring flyer in Korea. Lt Col Hinton also got his second, as did Col Meyer – the final Korean victories for both men. The 28th BS's hard-pressed B-29 crews added another laurel when gunner, Sgt Billy G Beach, was credited with two MiG-

Although B-29 crews came in for some rough treatment at the hands of MiG-15 pilots, who employed slashing attack tactics to make full use of their speed and height advantage, the remote barbette gunners in the Superfortresses occasionally got their own back. This B-29 of the Kadena-based 19th BG boasts two MiG kills alongside its growing tally of completed bombing missions – the outsize bomb symbols denote that this particular Superfortress had had its bomb-bay modified to carry the huge 'Tarzan' earthquake bomb (J B Stark)

15 kills. Single victories were credited to five more B-29 gunners, and to Sabre pilot Capt Howard M Lane (336th FIS).

At this juncture, MiG-15s were still being flown by Soviet air divisions belonging to the 64th Independent Fighter Aviation Corps. The Soviets respected their American adversaries, and were not above acknowledging their own mistakes, as Maj Gen Georgy Lobov was to recall later:

'The first Soviet MiG-15 pilots did not have enough combat experience. It was one thing to defeat F-51s and F-80s, and quite another to face the F-86. Soviet commander Evgeny Pepelyaev confirmed that pilots needed to sharpen their tactics. Of course, the main goal of Soviet fighter aviation was not the scores of Sabres shot down but, rather to neutralise the bombers. From this point of view, avoiding combat was justified.

'In 1951, the first phase of Soviet MiG-15 operations in Korea was

Still only a captain at this point, James Jabara of the 334th FIS/4th FIW began to come to prominence in the spring of 1951 as he steadily claimed a string of MiG kills. In this candid shot, he is seen holding his familiar blood red bonedome whilst conversing with a fellow 'Eagle' from his squadron at a damp Suwon. Behind him is the Sabre he used to down his first confirmed kill on 3 April 1951 *(Leo Fournier)*

completed. This first stage had been very hard; witness the fact that these men were honoured with the title Hero of the Soviet Union, the top Soviet military award, when they destroyed three or four enemy aircraft. Because this first group gained experience through great sacrifice, pilots who replaced them had it easier. The newer pilots were better trained, going to Korea as volunteers without illusions, prepared to confront an experienced opponent with a high-performance fighter.

'Rotating Soviet air units (rather than individuals) through the Korean conflict had an inherent flaw. New pilots went into combat without experienced colleagues beside them. Newcomers "stepped on the same rake" (a Russian phrase about repeating mistakes), sometimes smashing their faces in blood. Pilots who completed a tour of duty could only orally pass along their experience to newcomers. There was a decline in MiG activity after each turnaround of pilots, and one consequence was increased losses. The Americans, in contrast, rotated people, not squadrons. "Elders" coached newcomers as they gained experience.

'This rotation scheme typifies the way that Soviet leaders – both military and civil – approached any activity. If something did not succeed, shallow decisions, often not touching the cause of the problem, were usually taken. If F-86s won a battle with MiG-15s, pilots and commanders were to be blamed and replaced. The second group of pilots was selected more carefully than the first. No 324 Fighter Air Division under World War 2 ace Ivan Kozhedub, three times Hero of the Soviet Union, consisted of two regiments (Nos 196 Fighter Air Regiment and 176 Guard Fighter Air Regiment) and was composed of volunteers who had accumulated high hours (by Soviet standards) in jets, particularly in MiG-15s. Many veterans of the Great Patriotic War were among them.'

No 303 Fighter Air Division, under Lobov, was formed at the same time, and joined No 324 at airfields in Manchuria, flying from Antung.

MORE CORSAIRS

The Corsair pilots started building up a modest tally of aerial victories on 21 April 1951 when two F4Us from VMA-312 chanced upon a rare outing by North Korean Yak-9s. Capt Phillip C DeLong, a World War 2 ace with 11 kills, and 1st Lt Harold D Daigh were jumped by four Yaks near Chinnampo. The Corsair pilots out-manoeuvred the enemy and Lt Daigh quickly knocked one of the Yaks down with a burst from his .50 calibre guns. Capt DeLong then shot down two more while Lt Daigh damaged the remaining Yak as it made a run for safer skies to the north.

The gull-winged Corsair was the last US propeller-driven fighter in production, and was a truly great aeroplane. Powered by a 2250 hp Pratt & Whitney R-2800-42W radial engine in the case of the F4U-4 (most used in Korea), the Corsair was credited with a maximum speed of 395 mph at 20,000 ft. The air-cooled engine was a boon when fighting at low-level, where metal was flying around and survivability was a real issue. No less than 12,571 Corsairs were manufactured (the last being delivered in January 1953), and in Korea, versions employed included the F4U-4, F4U-4B, F4U-5, F4U-5N, F4U-5NL and F4U-5P.

Heavy fighting saw four MiG-15s shot down on 22 April 1951, Jabara achieving the unprecedented by bagging his fourth kill. Eagleston and Yancey each claimed their second, and final, victories of the war, whilst

1st Lt Richard S (Dick) Becker (334th FIS) scored his first. The high-scoring Jabara had not yet finished battling the MiG-15, however, as he was allowed to remain at Suwon after the 334th rotated back to Japan (one squadron stayed in the rear while two flew from Korean soil).

Except for brief flare-ups, fighting in MiG Alley dramatically subsided in the spring of 1951, just as a final spasm of terrain-swapping approached its end thousands of feet below. On 24 April, Lt Col William J Hovde of the 4th FIW headquarters flight shot down a MiG-15, which was to be the last aerial victory for four weeks. Hovde had earlier scored 10.5 kills with the Eighth Air Force in World War 2.

Meanwhile, FEAF officers agonised over whether the lumbering B-29 could hack it in skies where the MiG-15 came and went as it pleased. The FEAF's B-29 force was commanded by Maj Gen Emmett 'Rosie' O'Donnell, Jr, who had available both the 98th and 307th BGs, on loan from Strategic Air Command. These had replaced the 22nd and 92nd BGs, which had been on the scene at the war's beginning. In addition, O'Donnell had the 19th BG which had belonged to the FEAF all along. Each group, with three squadrons, was authorised 33 bombers, giving O'Donnell – on paper at least – 99 Superfortresses. But the MiG force kept whittling that number down, and morale in the units was dangerously low.

In April 1951, Gen Douglas MacArthur was relieved and replaced by Lt Gen Matthew B Ridgway. It was the most publicised sacking of an officer since the Civil War, and Truman expressed 'regret that General of the Army Douglas MacArthur is unable to give his wholehearted support to the policies of the United States government'.

The following month Jabara – now flying with the 335th FIS – racked up his fifth and sixth victories on the 20th in F-86A-5 49-1318. His achievement was all the greater because he was flying off balance at the time with a hung droptank.

At the age of 27, Jim Jabara was not merely an ace, but a seasoned World War 2 veteran. The son of a Wichita grocer, he claimed that the MiG could outrun and outclimb the F-86 above 30,000 ft. Jabara also said that he wished he had four 20 mm cannon instead of six .50 cals. The Sabre's A-4 radar-ranging gunsight was superior to the MiG's sighting system, and the former's 1802 rounds of ammunition stood a better chance of hitting something (despite inflicting less damage), but MiG pilots enjoyed heavier armour protection. Still, Jabara felt the F-86 was 'the best jet in the world, and the MiG the second best'.

With Jabara confirmed as the first ace, it could be said that the USAF had a simple kills accreditation system in place. However, it was by no means easy to be credited with an aerial victory. The rules for a confirmed kill were strict, and required at least two of the following – eyewitnesses, gun-camera film or a confirmed sighting of wreckage

VMA-312 had a hectic war, operating firstly from forward airfields close to the war zone, and then returning to seaborne duties from the light carrier USS *Bataan* (CVL-29). The vessel spent most of its time cruising in the Yellow Sea off the west coast of Korea, and tours alternated between ship and shore for the Marine Corsair units throughout the conflict. In spring 1951 the 'Checkerboards' spent three months aboard ship, and on 21 April 1951, three Yak-9s were destroyed by Capt Phillip C DeLong and Lt Harold D Daigh near Chinnampo. These F4U-4s are fully loaded with bombs and HVARs and await the signal to launch on yet another strike mission from *Bataan* in May 1951

on the ground. These requirements were far more rigid than those in place in Europe during World War 2 (where, among other things, aircraft destroyed on the ground were counted within the Eighth Air Force). There is agreement that the desire to 'make ace' strengthened morale, not just of pilots but of the crewchiefs and armourers who worked on the jets, but at times it also led to a breakdown of discipline and to needless casualties. The Pentagon states that the term 'ace' enjoyed no official sanction, but Jabara discovered that fellow officers treated him with the awe and deference usually reserved for Medal of Honor recipients.

The 'ace system' wasn't helped by the early gun cameras on Sabres either. 'There were all kinds of problems', remembers Martin J Bambrick, who got a MiG later in the war. 'The guy goes out to load the camera (fitted at the bottom of the nose air intake). He doesn't know whether there'll be a short between the camera and the guns. So the procedure is to check the circuit breaker in the cockpit. A lot of the time we had bad film, or it didn't run, got frozen or the Plexiglas in front got scratched.'

In at least one of the 4th FIW's squadrons, pilots became so 'MiG happy' that they ignored basic tactics, took risks, and, as happened intermittently, crossed the Yalu. Jabara, Becker, Gibson and others of this era later claimed that they shot down more MiGs than anyone said, but were faced with a dilemma – everybody wanted to be an ace, but nobody wanted to be relieved from combat for breaking the rules of engagement.

While American fighter pilots felt that their system for confirming aerial victories was both strict and harsh, Soviet pilots regarded the Americans as 'a bunch of softies'! According to Col Evgeny Pepelyaev, USAF claims 'were evidently exaggerated because some of these MiG-15s, seemingly shot down on the camera films of Sabres, actually landed at their airfield with damage. Soviet pilots had a stricter system of counting victories, with evidence from military men on the ground, or from civil authorities, as well as photo film and a report by the pilot and his squadron mates being required. If a UN aircraft downed by MiGs fell in territory where this confirmation was impossible, the kill was often not credited'. In fact, the Soviet system sounds identical to the American. Adds Pepelyaev, 'Not everything that was scored (on the Soviet side) was actually shot down!'

On the same day as Jabara's fifth kill, a MiG-15 was credited to Capt Milton E Nelson, a pilot from the 335th FIS. Three more MiGs fell on 31 May 1951, two to Sabre pilots and one to a B-29 gunner. The next day, two B-29 gunners and another F-86 pilot toted up additional MiG kills.

Also in May, the Royal Australian Air Force's (RAAF) No 77 Sqn retreated from Pusan to Iwakuni and began the transition from battle-weary Mustangs to Meteor F.8 twin-engine jet fighters. These machines were sent out directly from Britain aboard the carrier HMS *Warrior*, with later shipments of F.8s eventually arriving in Australia for domestic use.

An F-86 from the USAF was detached to Iwakuni to fly comparison tests with a Meteor and, in effect, to behave like a MiG. An argument boiled up between the USAF and the RAAF over how the Meteor should be used, with No 77's boss, Sqn Ldr Dick Cresswell, claiming that it should serve as an interceptor. This was the role eventually allocated to the unit, although there existed serious doubts in the American camp that the straight-winged Meteor could survive aloft with the MiG-15.

Lt Gen George E Stratemeyer, commander of the FEAF, suffered a

Following James Jabara's double MiG killing feat to become an ace on 20 May 1951, he returned to Suwon to discover that he had been vaulted into the position of most famous post-World War 2 pilot in the USAF up to that point in the Korean conflict. Media attention was immediate, and here he is seen posing at Johnson air base, in Japan, for a staged interview in front of the F-86A-5 (49-1318) he used to become an ace several days after the mission in question

heart attack in May 1951 and was replaced by Lt Gen Otto P Weyland, an ex-fighter pilot.

On 1 June, Lt Simpson Evans, a US Navy exchange pilot serving with an F-86 unit, was credited with a MiG-15 kill. Just over a fortnight later, on the 17th, an intruding Polikarpov Po-2LSh biplane dropped two bombs on Suwon. Some UN officers dismissed the mostly-canvas Po-2 as a nocturnal nuisance with no purpose except to annoy. Few Americans knew, however, that *Wehrmacht* troops on the Eastern Front during World War 2 feared the Po-2, and believed that its crew could 'look' into each window to see if soldiers were inside a house. By destroying one F-86A (49-1334), and seriously damaging eight more, this single incursion by 'Bedcheck Charlie' – the nickname given to the Po-2 – had inflicted far more harm to the Sabre force than the MiG-15 had so far achieved.

Po-2 crews seemed to mock the Americans. Their mount was difficult to detect on radar, and hard to spot with the naked eye. Capt Edwin B Long was aloft near Seoul on the night of 30 June when ground radar vectored him toward an intruder. Accompanied by radar operator, WO R C Buckingham, Long took his F7F-3N Tigercat north of the capital and began looking.

'The slow, very manoeuvrable, biplane was next to impossible to get a clean shot at. It took three passes for me to get him lined up. But when I did, the tremendous firepower of the Tigercat did the job quickly, and he went down into the side of a mountain in a fiery crash'. Long remembers that 'his' Po-2 was a black biplane with a radial engine, and he believes that he was fired upon from the rear cockpit by a hand-held weapon, probably a PPSh-41 7.62 mm 'burp' gun. The Tigercat pilot belonged to VMF(N)-513, the squadron known as the 'Flying Nightmares', which was now equipped with both F4U-5Ns and F7F-3Ns – he had just racked up the first victory of the conflict for Marine nightfighters.

The Tigercat was a shoulder-wing monoplane with outer wing panels that folded for carrier stowage. Though it flew for the first time in World War 2 (on 2 November 1943), the Tigercat was too late to see action in that war. Powered by two 2100 hp Pratt & Whitney R-2800-34W Double Wasp 18-cylinder engines, and capable of 435 mph at 22,200 ft, the Tigercat had a gross weight of 25,720 lb, which was less than some single-engined aircraft. The F7F-3 had four 20 mm cannon in the wing roots and four .50 cal machine-guns in the nose, and could carry up to 2000 lb of bombs. It never did serve on carrier decks but, along with the F4U-5N, was all-important to the USMC's war against 'Bedcheck Charlie' and other nocturnal activities.

At about the time of Tigercat pilot Long's night aerial victory, another 'Bedcheck Charlie' Po-2 (on 24 June 1951) blundered in front of a B-26 Invader flown by Capt Richard M Heyman of the 3rd BG. Heyman was an ex-fighter pilot, but even B-26 aircrew who *hadn't* flown fighters knew

that their bomber could be a real threat. Part of the 3rd's 8th BS (perhaps the most experienced outfit in Korea), Heyman responded to the Kimpo air direction centre's call for help, throttled down enough to get behind the Po-2, and blasted it out of the sky.

The RAAF's No 77 Sqn converted from the F-51D to the Meteor F.8 (with a T.7 trainer or two also on board) in the early months of 1951. At first, there were hopes that the Meteor could handle the MiG-15, but the British-designed fighter proved to be no match for the Russian fighter in a dogfight. Soviet literature claimed that Russian MiG-15 pilots flying from Manchuria once shot down a dozen Meteors in a day, which was probably more than the unit ever got into the air at once! This view shows an early F.8 sitting alongside one of the last F-51Ds on the squadron's books. Photographed in March 1951 at Pusan, A77-982 was infact the highest serial given to a Meteor in RAAF service – the jet was lost during a ground-attack sortie in June 1953 *(George J Busher)*

Another shot of -982, this time in company with F.8 A77-368 and T.7 A77-305. Seen cruising at height along the Korea west coast, -368 survived the war (one of only three of the original batch of 14 F.8s sent to Korea to do so) and is now held in storage with the Australian War Memorial. Ironically, the T.7 is also a survivor (re-serialled as -702), and is presently on display at the RAAF Museum in Point Cook, Victoria *(via Aeroplane)*

After a single kill by a Sabre on 17 June 1951, five MiG-15s fell to F-86 pilots on 18 June. Maj Richard D Creighton (336th FIS), who'd established a world speed record in the Sabre in 1948, racked up his first kill, and 1st Lt Ralph D 'Hoot' Gibson went one better by opening his account with two MiGs. On 20 June, F-51 pilot 1st Lt James B Harrison (67th FBS/18th FBW) bagged a Yak-9, whilst in addition to Heyman's Po-2 kill, single MiG-15s were shot down by Sabre pilots on 24, 25 and 26 June 1951.

A look at the situation at the end of June showed grim statistics for UN pilots. The Chinese – increasingly taking over flying duties from the Russians – now possessed 445 MiGs, opposed by a mere 44 F-86As then on strength with the 4th FIW in Korea. While the Americans were clearly outnumbered, the situation was even worse than it looked, with Col Herman A Schmid, who had replaced Col George F Smith as the 4th's boss observing that it took 'maintenance miracles' to keep *half* of his Sabres in the air. While Schmid appeared to be outnumbered ten-to-one, his Sabres actually faced a *twenty-to-one* disadvantage, vis-a-vis the Chinese.

Deliveries of the MiG-15bis with improved performance began in the summer of 1951. This new marque was powered by a 5952 lb thrust Klimov VK-1 engine which boosted its maximum speed to 677 mph at 10,000 ft. The MiG-15bis also introduced changes in wiring, hydraulics and cockpit layout, which made it a more effective air-to-air fighter.

Three of the USAF's most capable Sabre pilots racked up MiG-15 aerial victories on 8 July. Col Francis S Gabreski, commander of the 4th FIW's 4th FIG, was the 'old man' of the trio. The top living US ace had scored 28 kills with the 61st FS/56th FG in Europe, and he had now claimed his first in Korea. 1st Lt Richard S Becker bagged his second MiG, whilst the least known of the trio was Maj Franklin L Fisher of the 4th FIW HQ Flight – this was his first success.

July also saw Capt Milton E Nelson (335th FIS) shoot down his second MiG-15 and 'Hoot' Gibson his third. B-29 gunner Sgt Gus C Opfer of the 3rd BS was credited with two MiGs. On 29 July, F-80C pilot 1st Lt William W McAllister (16th FIS/51st FIW) claimed a MiG-15. On 8 August 1951, 1st Lt Richard S Becker claimed two MiGs to double his score. There was certainly 'ace fever' in his 334th FIS, but there was also restraint – years later Becker claimed that both he and other

A dramatic sketch of VMF(N)-513's first Tigercat kill of the Korean conflict, as drawn by Sgt Tom Murray (an enlisted man in the unit) literally hours after the combat. The pilot of the F7F-3N on this flight was Capt Edwin B Long, who was ably assisted in the night intercept by radar operator, WO R C Buckingham

The Tigercat really was an awesome weapon of war, and in all honesty possessed an embarrassing excess of firepower when it came to dealing with the North Korean 'Bedcheck Charlie' Po-2s that proved to be the F7F's main target

pilots had downed MiGs which were never credited.

The Australians also had their first MiG encounter in August 1951, Sqn Ldr Dick Wilson diving behind one jet, only to be hit by cannon fire from another. A shell penetrated his rear fuselage, bounced around, and punctured the main fuel tank. The Meteor's port aileron was also virtually shot away, but somehow he mustered extraordinary skill and nursed his damaged F.8 (A77-616) back to Kimpo – this jet was later lost to ground fire in February 1952. Less fortunate was the pilot of A77-721, WO Ron Guthrie, who was shot down by a MiG and made a PoW.

The Australian pilot had had his elevators shot away on the MiGs' first pass, throwing his F.8 into an uncontrollable rolling dive at Mach 0.84. As his jet passed through 38,000 ft he ejected, and a full 28 minutes later came down in a paddy field. Guthrie's ejection was only the fifth ever performed by a Martin-Baker seat in an emergency, and the first under fire. It also set a record at that time for the highest ejection from an aircraft, plus the longest descent. He was finally repatriated in late 1953.

On 24 August MiGs were shot down by Col Benjamin S Preston, Jr (4th FIW), and Capt Jack A Robinson (334th FIS), whilst on 2 September, 22 F-86s battled 40 MiGs in a half-hour duel which raged between Sinuiju and Pyongyang – they shot down four, which were credited to Gabreski (his second), Gibson (his fourth), Capt Richard S Johns and Maj Winton W 'Bones' Marshal. A week later a pitched duel was fought between 28 F-86s and 70 MiGs, newly-promoted Capts Richard S Becker and Ralph D 'Hoot' Gibson each claiming their fifth kills to become the second and third US aces.

The 'top brass' were trying to use their meagre F-86 strength to keep MiGs away from bomber formations, although through sheer weight of numbers the latter were often getting through. F-84Es of the 8th FBS/49th FBW on a bombing sortie were bounced by six MiGs near Sukchon on 10 September. Their flight leader, 1st Lt William Skliar, describes what happened next.

'We were on a rail cutting mission. After our bomb runs, we were rejoining when the MiGs dove down on us. I called a break into the lead MiG and when he saw us turn he reversed direction. At that moment, another MiG came across my path in a rapid turn about 1200 ft in front of me. I laid my "Hog" (as the F-84 was nicknamed) into as tight a turn as possible and managed to draw a lead. We were at near max range for our .50s, but I got some good long bursts in. After a glance around to check where the other MiGs were, mine just disappeared. Knowing that the enemy often tried to decoy us

The B-26 Invader found itself in several air-to-air scrapes during the war, including one in which pilot 1st Lt Robert W Fox hosed off several bursts of fire from the bomber's nose guns at a fleeing MiG-15. On 24 June 1951 a Po-2LSh blundered in front of a B-26B flown by Capt Richard M Heyman of the 3rd BG's 8th BS, and he blasted it out of the sky. It was the only official B-26 kill of the war. This B-26B was one of the aircraft assigned to 'The Liberty Squadron' at the time of the shootdown *(John Sidirourgos)*

1st Lt Charles 'Chazz' Herron of the 51st FIW wasn't a MiG killer, but this F-80C (49-607) nevertheless wears a red star. It's possible that -607 was flown by 1st Lt William W McAllister of the Wing's 16th FIS when he shot down a MiG on 29 July 1951. The 51st scored just two victories (both MiGs) whilst flying the F-80, although one source indicates that as many as five 51st FIW Shooting Stars had kills painted on them! *(USAF)*

into chasing them, I backed off in favour of getting everyone back together. At least I had the satisfaction of knowing that some of their decoys had almost bought the farm. I was credited with a "probable".'

Fourteen MiGs and three F-86s went down in air-to-air fighting in September. The favourable kill ratio was a cruel and misleading statistic. Able to fight only when and where the enemy chose, outnumbered F-86 pilots felt that the MiG-15 was slowly getting the better of them.

On 19 September, Thunderjet pilot Capt Kenneth L Skeen (9th FBS/49th FBW) shot down the first MiG-15 credited to his outfit after being forced to jettison his bombs and abandon an air-to-ground sortie. Skeen's later described it in the following account.

'We were on a strike by the entire 49th Group against a rail complex located between Sinanju and Pyongyang. Each unit used 16 jets, and total ordnance was 96 500 lb general purpose bombs. Since I was one of the new pilots, I would be flying in the number four position in the last flight. My call sign was "Purple 4". As we passed east of Pyongyang, I heard the Group leader call in MiGs at one o'clock high. For the past few minutes we'd been listening to the controller calling out "MiG trains heading south". We assumed the F-86s would be in a position to intercept them, but unknown to us they were still on the ground at Kimpo and we were on our own! There was a lot of radio chatter, with calls of "MiGs at three o'clock high! They're coming in! Salvo your bombs! Get up some speed!" Then came the dreaded, "Break right, 'Purple' flight!"

'Being the last man in the flight, I was just hanging on as we went to full throttle. The MiGs overshot their attacking turn and I pulled up high to our left, as "Purple" leader reversed the turn hard to the left into the MiGs. Since I was on the outside of the turn, I started falling behind. As I cut across to the inside to catch up with Maj Jim Sprinkle – my element leader – who was far ahead of me, a blue MiG-15 dropped down in front of me and locked onto Sprinkle's tail. The enemy pilot evidently never saw me as he was busy lining up the F-84 in his sights. He was decelerating to get a better shot, while I was at full throttle to catch up. I lined up the gunsight on him, took my feet off the rudder pedals to make sure the aircraft was flying true, and squeezed the trigger.

'I gave him a long burst of .50 calibre API (Armour Piercing Incendiary). Immediately, pieces started flying off of the MiG, accompanied by smoke and flames. As he slowed, I saw that he was on fire and I pulled to his left to keep from running into him. He went into the thin undercast as I glanced to my left and saw another blue MiG right on the tail of another F-84. I yelled, "F-84! Break! Break! MiG on your tail! Break right!", hoping to bring the MiG into my sights. As the F-84 broke, the MiG pulled up high to the left. I looked back to my right as I entered the thin undercast and saw a parachute descending, but not a single jet in sight. I climbed back on top to find the sky deserted where just moments before there has been a mass of aircraft. With my fuel showing well below bingo level, I headed south for the base at K-2. The rail cutting mission had been unsuccessful as we jettisoned our bomb loads, but all jets returned, with only one damaged. Most importantly, the 9th had scored its first kill!'

A further 5.5 MiG-15s were credited to F-86 pilots in September 1951, but the 'bandit trains', or large formations, attacking from sanctuary north of the Yalu, continued to enjoy the initiative in the fight. Lt Gen Weyland felt the outnumbered F-86 force was taking it on the chin. He warned the Pentagon that the Chinese 'may be able to establish bases in Korea and threaten our air supremacy over the front lines'. It was to no avail. In Washington Gen Vandenberg was told that no more F-86s could be despatched to Korea. On 20 September he informed Weyland that the means did not exist to support a second Sabre wing in Korea.

On 23 September an F7F-3N of VMF(N)-513, flown by Maj E A Van Gundy and Master Sergeant T H Ullom, was searching for a Po-2, and soon made radar contact. The pilot went down to minimum speed to avoid overshooting his quarry, and at a range of 500 ft, Van Gundy spotted the Po-2 and fired 100 rounds of 20 mm ammunition at it before he overshot. The Polikarpov burst into flames and crashed.

The conflict was now permanently stalemated on the ground, but not in the air. The size and scope of the fighting along MiG Alley was altered dramatically in October 1951, one of the busiest months of the war. The outnumbered 4th FIW fought the biggest jet air battles in history over northwestern Korea, some of them involving hundreds of jet fighters. The MiG force had now increased to 525 aircraft, but was still opposed by just 44 F-86A. Not phased by these odds, the 4th continued to whittle down this huge force, destroying two MiGs on 1 October, six on 2 October, one on 5 October, one on 12 October and no fewer than *nine* MiGs (the biggest daily score yet) on 16 October.

The heightened level of aerial fighting was also marked by savage MiG attacks on B-29s. On 23 October 1951, as Superforts went after targets in the north, 100 MiGs engaged and boxed in the 34 Sabres of the screening force. The F-86 pilots shot down two MiGs, but this

The Meteor F.8 was quickly shown to be unable to hold its own with the MiG-15, and was soon relegated to ground attack tasks. The jet closest to the camera (A77-862, which was written off in a mid-air collision with A77-866 in Korea in May 1954) wears the title *THE DUKE OF BATH* below the cockpit, whilst the jet farthest from the photographer (A77-864, which crash landed at Kimpo in February 1954) boasts a squadron commander's pennant below its cockpit (*Alan Royston via Tony Fairbairn*)

4th FIG boss Col Francis S Gabreski congratulates the second and third US aces in Korea, Capt Richard S Becker (left) and 1st Lt Ralph 'Hoot' Gibson, after they each downed their fifth MiG during the monumental dogfight over the Yalu on 9 September 1951 [USAF]

was no comfort to the eight B-29 crews arrayed in three flights, and escorted by 55 F-84s. Fifty MiGs got through and attacked the bomber force. A Thunderjet-versus-MiG fray on the edges of the formation proved little, except that the F-84 was not MiG-killer material.

While this struggle went on, two more B-29s were shot down. In fact, all but one of the bombers received major damage and most had casualties aboard when they diverted for emergency landings at forward airfields. It was the blackest day in the history of the medium bomber force, and it proved that daylight raids on North Korea had to end.

Capt Kenneth L Skeen of the 9th FBS/49th FBW is helped on with his straps prior to departing from Taegu (K-2) on a strike mission in his MiG-killing F-84E. His was the first aerial victory for the wing, and came on 19 September 1951 after his strike formation had been bounced by MiGs east of Pyongyang. Skeen's MiG is painted in plan view just forward of his flashy nameplate below the cockpit

One F-86 pilot scoring regularly in the latter stages of 1951 was 1st Lt Hal Fischer (on the left) of the 4th's 39th FIS, who achieved the rare distinction of downing two MiGs in one day on 16 October. Few shark's mouths were applied to F-86s in Korea, thus making Fischer's ferocious looking Sabre something of a rarity amongst other 4th FIW jets *(Harold Fischer)*

Russian MiG-15 pilots refer to this slaughter of B-29s as 'Black Tuesday'. To Maj Gen Lobov, the date 'meant nothing more and nothing less than the complete collapse of USAF strategic aviation'. Lobov accuses American authors of 'a tendency to play down their losses and to emphasise the unlikely high number of Soviet fighters participating in the battles, and their mythical losses. This was done to maintain the tarnished prestige of US military aviation, to placate the public and to conceal the coarsest mistakes of their command, the shortcomings of equipment and the extremely low spirits of the B-29 crews'. *Newsweek* magazine reported that US bomber losses on 'Black Tuesday' were '100 per cent'. According to Lobov, 'not one bomb' fell where it was supposed to.

The USAF drew little comfort from the fact that B-29 gunners claimed five MiG-15s and an F-84 pilot a sixth. The latter kill was accomplished by Navy Lt (and future astronaut) Walter M Schirra, flying on exchange. An F-84E was downed in return by a MiG in the middle of the fighting.

The communists destroyed another Superfortress the following day despite an escort of 16 Meteors and 10 F-84s. The impact that the Russian pilots had on the B-29s was as dramatic as they later claimed. Unable to survive against the MiG in daylight, the bombers switched to night raids after the heavy losses of October, which the Russians claim added up to 12 B-29s and four F-84 – the official USAF figure was eight and one.

A COLONEL'S WAR

When Col Harrison R (Harry) Thyng took command of the embattled 4th FIW at Kimpo on 1 November 1951 (replacing Schmid), he was one of the most experienced combat pilots in the USAF. Thyng's first fighter had

been a Spitfire, and he'd racked up kills in both Europe and the Pacific. His gift was 'leadership and courage', as his orderly room chief, Staff Sergeant Gordon Beem remembers. Others recall Thyng's lack of interest in glory for himself – he often gave away his kills to other pilots.

Col Thyng arrived in Korea as the first cohort of American fighter pilots was finishing up and going home. Like these veterans, some of the new arrivals had fought in World War 2, but unlike them, these older heads had gotten out of uniform, launched careers and started families. They'd been recalled involuntarily; their average age was 30 to 32; they'd already done their part in the most horrific war the world had ever known; and they resented this new war as an intrusion into their lives.

Reporting aboard in Col Thyng's orderly room at Kimpo along with the disgruntled older veterans were a new breed – fresh pilots in their early twenties, taught to fly in 1950 and 1951. The new men were quick of reflex, less bitter, and unfettered by bad habits. Harry Thyng had jumped from props to jets without blinking, but Col Gabreski, for example, couldn't get the hang of the F-86's gunsight, and was aiming at MiGs through chewing-gum wadded on his windscreen! In contrast, a 25-year-old 'balloon' (new second lieutenant) like James F Low could tweak up the Sabre's A-4 radar-ranging gunsight and use it as naturally as an extension of his own eyes and hands. Thyng wrote that 'the proper use of the gunsight was something that needed to be emphasised more'.

Two generations of fighter pilots are covered in this shot of 1st Lt James F Low (left), the most junior ace of the war (though not the youngest), and Col Harrison Thyng (right), boss of the 4th FIW, who achieved acedom in two conflicts. Young fighter jocks like Low got most of the attention, and had films made about them, but it was the experienced Col Thyng who bore the burden of command *(James F Low)*

He saw his pilots hamstrung by maintenance problems and outnumbered by the MiGs, so he decided to risk his new job by waving a flag of warning in the face of the Air Force Chief of Staff in the Pentagon. He sent a message in November which leapfrogged his superiors and flaunted the chain of command. The key sentences read, 'PERSONAL TO VANDENBERG FROM THYNG. I CAN NO LONGER BE RESPONSIBLE FOR AIR SUPERIORITY IN NORTHWEST KOREA.'

On 4 November, USMC Capt William F Guss, flying an F-86 on exchange, shot down a MiG. Four days later, Maj William T Whisner, Jr, of the 334th FIS, shot down two MiG-15s along the Yalu. These kill was added to his Eighth Air Force tally of 15.5 from seven years before.

On 18 November, MiG-15s sneaked up on the F-84 flown by 1st Lt William Coward of the 111th FBS/136th FBW and riddled it with gunfire. Coward was able to nurse the jet out to the Yellow Sea, before bailing out. Two other 111th FBS pilots, 1st Lts Kenneth C Cooley and John M Hewett, Jr, evened the score for the day, however, by sharing a MiG kill. 18 November was also the date when no fewer than three MiG were shot down by Navy carrier-based Panther pilots – Lt Cdr W E Lamb, Lt R E Parker and Ens F C Weber.

Half of the successful VMF(N)-513 duo who claimed a Po-2 on 23 September 1951 models for a Christmas snap to be sent home. RO, MSgt Tom H Ullom, stands in the middle of this happy trio, who have chosen an unconventional canvas on which to paint their festive greeting. Immediately behind them is a nose radar-equipped F7F-3N, which boasts a rather unusual high-viz code number *(Tom Ullom)*

51st FIGHTER INTERCEPTOR WING

After Col Harry Thyng's call, USAF chief of staff Gen Vandenberg continued to be reticent about shipping more Sabres to Korea for about a month. Then, on 22 October 1951, he issued a controversial order to the Air Defense Command to send 75 F-86A/Es with pilots and crew chiefs to Alameda, California, to be loaded aboard an escort carrier for Japan.

The way was paved to equip the 51st FIW at Suwon with Sabres, initially with two units (16th and 25th), whilst the beleaguered 4th FIW was to get its third squadron.

On 27 November 1951, pilots from the 4th FIW shot down four MiGs, one of the victors being Maj Richard D Creighton, who became the war's fourth American ace on this day. He was a jet pioneer, and a much-respected leader and tactician who'd flown the F-86A to a speed record immediately before the start of the war. Two other MiG kills were credited to Maj George A Davis, Jr, boss of the 334th FIS, and another pioneer who'd flown with the USAF's first Sabre wing before the war, and was highly respected for his aggressive spirit and tactical skills. The following day, 'Bones' Marshal scored his second and third MiG kills. Another kill, greatly helped by Col Thyng coaxing the MiG into the right place, was credited to 1st Lt Dayton W Ragland, one of the USAF's first black pilots.

On 30 November 1951, 31 Sabres led by Col Benjamin S Preston, the 4th FIW's group commander, came upon a formation of 12 twin-engined Tupolev Tu-2 bombers, 16 La-9 propeller-driven fighters and 16 MiG-15s. This may have been an attempt to revive the North Korean air force, as UN intelligence had detected attempts to open the airfield at Uiju, south of the Yalu, and had monitored radio chatter in Korean rather than Chinese. The gaggle of aircraft found two flights of Sabres swarming

No less than 25 F-86Es can be seen in this view of the flightdeck of the carrier USS *Cape Esperance*. This shot was taken in mid-Pacific in the summer of 1951, and upon their arrival in Korea these jets were shared between the 4th and the formerly F-80-equipped 51st FIWs. A typical wing in-theatre boasted roughly 65 F-86s split between three squadrons *(Harry Dawson)*

down on them, firing and missing. When the Sabres re-engaged, an La-9 went down, then a Tu-2.

Maj Davis added to his existing credits by claiming a Tu-2, then picked off an unwary MiG to become the war's fifth American ace. Maj Winton W 'Bones' Marshal destroyed a Tu-2 and a La-9 to become the sixth jet ace, whilst other bombers were shot out the sky by 1st Lts Robert W Akin, John J Burke and Douglas K Evans, and

Capt Raymond O Barton, Jr. Further La-9s were claimed by Col Preston (his fourth and final Korean War kill) and 1st Lt John W Honaker.

Today, the wartime survivors of No 77 Sqn are unlikely to have forgotten 1 December 1951, a date that saw no fewer than 14 Meteor F.8s head north to fight. While two jets in 'Stovepipe Dog' flight orbited near Pyongyang to act as airborne relays, three flights of four Meteors each, using the call signs 'ANZAC Able', 'Baker' and 'Charlie', headed deep into MiG country. This late-morning foray wrote a bittersweet fable of the Meteor's first aerial victory, coupled with combat losses. The following report also highlights the confusion typical of air combat.

'"Able", "Baker" and "Charlie" flights were flying at a heading of 070 degrees at 19,000 ft. About 40 MiG-15s were overhead. Two attacked "Charlie 3" and "4" from six o'clock, while two more came in from the rear at "Baker" flight. "Able 1" held his break, then broke after a pair of MiGs and fired with no obvious result. "Able 3" held his break with "Able 1" and observed one Meteor from "Charlie" flight in a hard starboard turn, streaming fuel.' As we shall soon learn from this account, 'Able 3' was very busy during the mission. Behind the callsign, wedged into A77-15's cockpit, was Flg Off Bruce Gogerly, an ex-Kittyhawk pilot from World War 2. '"Able 3" slackened the break, still in a starboard turn, and the two MiGs which had attacked "Charlie" flight loomed up ahead.

'"Able 3" left "Able 1" and followed the MiGs in a port turn at 800 yards range, firing a two-second burst with no obvious result. The MiGs steepened the turn, but "Able 3" pulled inside, closed to 500 yards and fired for five seconds, observing strikes on the rear fuselage and starboard wing root. The MiG pulled up to the left streaming fuel. "Able 3" broke off the attack when two other MiGs got on his tail. A couple of head-on passes were made with this pair and then "Able 3" turned starboard into two more MiGs coming in from nine o'clock. "Able 3" turned to port and fired a quick burst with no result and the MiGs broke off.

'"Able 3" and "4" then found themselves alone. "Able 3" then sighted an aircraft go down in flames and hit the top of a hill. Then

Although not of stunning quality, this photograph is nevertheless of some historical significance as it shows a three-ship of 51st FIW F-86Es carrying out one of their very first combat patrols over MiG Alley in early December 1951. The only unit markings then worn by the wing at Suwon were the yellow fuselage stripe and a suitably coloured intake lip surround, although not all Sabres exhibited the latter (via Jerry Scutts)

A77-207 (formerly WE905 of the RAF) was one of a handful of F.8s to wear nose art, boasting a red devil and the nickname 'Bowl 'em Over!' beneath the windscreen on the port side. This jet was the personal mount of the squadron's first MiG killer, Flg Off Bruce Gogerly, although it wasn't used by him during the torrid 1 December 1951 clash with MiG-15s that brought him success – Gogerly was flying A77-15 on this occasion. 'Bowl 'em Over!' survived the Korean War only to become a U.21A target drone at the Woomera missile range in South Australia, where it was finally destroyed by a projectile in November 1971 (Sherman Tandvig)

a lone MiG was sighted about 2000 yards ahead and 4000 to 5000 ft below; "ABLE 3" closed on him to 1200 yards in a dive down to an altitude of 14,000 ft. The MiG turned to port and flew level at 14,000 ft , then straightened out on a northerly heading and began to climb. "Able 3" held him for five seconds and fired a quick burst. The MiG rolled to port, recovered, and drew away. "Able 3" observed another aircraft go down in flames and strike the ground.

'"Baker 1" broke early over the formation followed by "Able 3", but was attacked by two MiGs from the rear; he broke south and climbed into the sun to 27,000 ft. The MiGs broke off their attack. "Baker 2" called that he had lost "Baker 1". However, "Baker 1" sighted an aircraft go down in flames from 24,000 ft and also noticed two Meteors being chased by two MiGs in a tight turn, range about 200-300 yards.

'"Baker 1" moved in to attack but was attacked by more MiGs and went down to 10,000 ft . One MiG followed down firing, then pulled away. After the break, "Baker 1" sighted a MiG pull up with fuel streaming. "Able 1" called a squadron check and all answered except "Baker 2". "Baker 1" called him twice and received an answer to the second call. "Baker 1" climbed to 30,000 ft and withdrew. "Baker 3" sighted what he thought to be a Meteor, zig-zagging down, streaming black smoke. This was about three minutes before the squadron radio check. The aircraft exploded at about 12,000 ft and crashed. "Baker 4" observed fuel streaming from one of the "Charlie" flight aircraft after the first break. He also observed two aircraft flame down before the squadron check.

'"Charlie 3" reported MiGs attacking and "Charlie 1" called the starboard break. "Charlie 3" and "4" were seen to break late and were not seen again. "Charlie 1" and "2" were attacked by two MiGs in a high port quarter attack. "Charlie 2" was hit in this attack. "Charlie 1" got behind two MiGs at 3000 yards range and fired at the starboard jet with no result.

'Then two MiGs attacked from the starboard high quarter. "Charlie 1" evaded them and then observed two Meteors being attacked by two MiGs close behind in a tight turn. He went in to attack but was attacked by more MiGs; after evading these he found himself about five miles north of the flight with seven MiGs. He dived to 7500 ft in compressibility and pulled out at 6000 ft. The MiGs pressed the attack to 7000 ft, still firing. "Baker 1" came out alone, and saw two fires on the ground near the positions given of the crashes above, well before the radio check was called.

'In the radio check "Charlie 4" reported he was streaming fuel and had no electrics. In the second break "Charlie 2" was hit and flicked, pulling out at 12,500ft, with altimeter, air speed and Mach gauges reading zero. Before the radio check he saw a jet falling in two burning pieces and crashing on a hill north of Pyongyang. He also observed a fire several miles north of this crash. Then one MiG attacked "Charlie 2" at 10,000 ft. He broke right and the MiG did not press the attack.

A war-weary veteran that served, and survived, No 77 Sqn's entire Meteor tour in Korea, A77-446 was eventually scrapped in Australia in April 1959. During its time in the frontline it was flown for a spell by Plt Off Ken Murray, hence its nickname, *Black Murray* *(via Aeroplane)*

'Two MiGs are claimed destroyed, one by "Able 3" (Gogerly, who had just scored the RAAF's first jet-versus-jet kill) and one which would appear to be a credit to the squadron as a whole. Three Meteors failed to return to base – "Baker 2" (Sgt B Thompson, in Meteor A77-29), "Charlie 3" (Flt Sgt E Armitt in A77-949) and "Charlie 4" (Sgt Vance Drummond in A77-251).' Thompson and Drummond ejected and spent the rest of the war as prisoners – they were both later killed in peacetime RAAF flying accidents, the former whilst at the controls of a Sabre, and the latter in a Mirage IIIO. Armitt died in the fight.

Elsewhere on 1 December 1951, 2nd Lt Robert E Smith, a fledgling F-80C Shooting Star pilot of the 36th FBS/8th FBW, shot down a MiG-15, whilst Col Gabreski (who had moved from the 4th) began F-86 operations at the helm of the second Sabre wing in Korea, the 51st at Suwon. According to original Sabre member Kenneth F Rhodes, 'We made the transition from F-80C to F-86E so fast that the engines never shut down'. The 51st bypassed the F-86A completely, receiving factory-fresh E-models. The first victory credited to the wing was a MiG-15 bagged by 1st Lt Paul E Roach (25th FIS/51st FIW) the day after their inaugural patrol.

YELLOW BANDS

Group commander, Lt Col George Jones, recognised that the 51st needed distinctive markings on its aircraft. To prevent F-86 Sabre pilots from mistaking each other for MiGs, the old hands at the 4th FIW had been flying with forward-slanting black-and-white stripes on the centre fuselage – similar to 'D-Day invasion stripes' worn by Allied aircraft almost a decade before – since way back in 1950. Jones didn't want to copy their stripes, so he set about designing something different.

Capt Ed Matczak, group materiel officer and budding artist, used grease pencils to draw a picture of an F-86 with a rearward-slanting yellow band on the fuselage, and yellow bands on the wing and tail. They were more attractive than the rival 4th's paint job, and they ended up being 28 inches wide on the fuselage (and swept back diagonally), and 36 inches wide on the wing, with a 4-inch black border in both locations.

Matczak's bands looked better and made it easier for UN pilots to distinguish a Sabre from a MiG. Col Walker H 'Bud' Mahurin, the World War 2 P-47 ace who joined the 51st some months after the bands had been applied, claimed that they were designed to set the Wing apart from the 4th, and to increase flagging morale. Later, the 51st revived the World War 2 markings pioneered by its 25th FS when it adorned the tails of its jets with black squares, thus becoming the 'Checkertails'.

The canvas for all these markings, the F-86E, provided something more substantial than a coat of paint to help boost flagging morale, however. was a giant step forward. By now, this version, with the 'all flying tail', was becoming standard, and pilots praised the way

Displaying definitive 51st FIW markings in this crisp shot is F-86E-1-NA 50-0649, here parked away in its revetment at Suwon. Nicknamed *Aunt Myrna* by its regular pilot, Walt Copeland, it also wears a thin red band above the distinctive chequered tail markings, thus denoting its allegiance to the 25th FIS. Copeland scored a single kill in this jet *(Walt Copeland)*

it manoeuvred with the MiG. Still, they were, as an official report at the time said, 'almost invariably outnumbered' by 'extreme odds'. MiG Alley itself was 'at the outer range of the F-86E's combat radius' and 'is over enemy territory at all times'.

Furthermore, even the worthy F-86E could not fully satisfy hard-working groundcrews. Daniel Walker, crew chief for 51st pilot Capt Iven C Kincheloe, noticed that the aileron actuators leaked (a glitch peculiar to the F-86E model) and, when the worst happened, all of the hydraulic fluid in the jet would gush out. When the aft section of the Sabre had to be removed for engine work, the spiral disconnectors were difficult to loosen or tighten properly. The canopy seal was never right. Further, even in the E-model, designers had not yet fixed a nose wheel which was too weak, and collapsed easily. Men like Walker had to cope with a difficult supply situation which was partly responsible for Thyng's complaint. Even if these problems could be solved, the 4th FIW alone could not handle hundreds of MiGs. Though new F-86s were constantly arriving, the aircraft-out-of-commission rate spiralled rapidly upward.

Despite their difficulties, Sabre pilots managed to shoot down 31 MiG-15s in December 1951, in addition to the MiG bagged by F-80C pilot, 2nd Lt Robert E Smith (36th FBS/8th FBW). One of the kills went to Maj Zane S Amell, much respected commander of the 4th Wing's 335th FS. Two MiG-15s fell to Maj George Davis, whilst Cols Preston and Thyng each added one to their respective scores. 1st Lt Paul Roach, who'd flown with both the 4th and 51st Wings, also racked up his third and final MiG kill during the month. Although now more outnumbered than ever before due to increases in MiG strength north of the Yalu, US pilots also felt they were seeing a steady deterioration in flight discipline by the 'bandit trains' scrambled against them – the Chinese were taking over from the Russians.

6 January 1952 was a day of heavy dogfighting along the Yalu River and F-86E pilots from the 51st FIW were awarded five kills, including one each for Col 'Bud' Mahurin and Maj William T Whisner, Jr.

That month, a staggering 45 per cent of all F-86s in Korea had to be listed as out of commission, 16.6 per cent for want of parts and 25.9 per cent because of maintenance problems. With two Sabre wings flying combat, the need for external fuel tanks jumped, and supply levels of these essential, but often expend-

Also assigned to the 51st FIW at about the same time as *Aunt Myrna* was *My Best Bett*, alias F-86E 50-0598. The mount of 2nd Lt Bernard Vise, this jet wears the blue tail stripe of the 16th FIS, as well as drab olive drop tanks, whose colour served to denote that they were built under contract in Japan – they possessed such different separation characteristics from the North American store when jettisoned that pilots had to be made aware of which type of tank they were carrying into combat *(Bernard Vise)*

A groundcrewmen get to grips with a minor glitch in the ammunition belt feed system on this distinctively (red) striped 25th FIS F-86E. Obviously mechanics of the highest order, a positive statement on the overall operability of this jet's six Brownings is made by the row of 7.5 red stars beneath the cockpit *(via Jerry Scutts)*

able, store were nearly exhausted come January. Many pilots were forced to fly combat patrols with only one wing tank, thus reducing patrol time.

The numbers of both communist and Allied warplanes in the skies along the North Korean border kept going up. In January 1952, MiG-15 'bandit trains' surging across the Yalu often numbered 100 aircraft, pilots using their high-altitude advantage by flying at 50,000 ft and jockeying into position to 'bounce' the Americans at Mach 0.9. The 4th Wing still flew mostly older F-86As, and although these were slightly faster than the newer, more manoeuvrable, F-86Es, all of the wing's flight leaders flew E-models. This essentially meant that the bulk of the 4th's pilots had difficulty getting high enough, fast enough, in their battle-weary F-86As to take away the enemy's advantage in the critical first moments of a fight. By contrast, the 51st had new F-86Es and could swarm into MiG Alley at speed (perhaps a few mph slower than the A-model, but no slower than the enemy), attacking from near-comparable altitudes with the MiGs.

As previously mentioned, there were signs that the general skill-level of the MiG pilots was decreasing as thier numbers increased – perhaps this was because fewer of them were Russians. In several engagements, 51st pilots caught the MiGs from behind, broke up their ragged formations, and shot them down. For example, in January 31 MiGs were destroyed for the loss of just five Sabres. All but a half-dozen of the kills were racked up by pilots in the second wing to operate Sabres, the 51st.

At about this time, several pilots in a flight of USAF F-86s claimed that they'd been 'stalked' by a Sabre flown by a communist pilot and adorned with red stars – the first of three such reports known to the authors. Like the earlier reports of the communist side flying F-63 Kingcobra fighters, the alleged sightings of a communist F-86 in the combat theatre were almost certainly not accurate. Due to Russian files having now been laid open, we know in retrospect that the communists *did* salvage a lightly damaged F-86 which had crashed in North Korea, ship it back to the Soviet Union, and carry out a series of test flights in the Moscow region, probably at the airfield known to the Allies as Ramanskoye. No information from the former Soviet Union, however, indicates that either they, the Chinese or the North Koreans ever flew an F-86 in combat.

On 10 February, Maj George Davis, the leading ace of the war at that stage with 12 victories, in addition to seven kills from World War 2, tore into a MiG 'bandit train' at 32,000 ft near the Yalu, just in time to prevent the MiGs from bouncing some Allied bombers. Davis wracked his F-86E (51-2725) around in a tight turn to close on the MiGs, and quickly achieved his final (13th and 14th) kills. Within seconds, however, a MiG pulled in tightly behind his Sabre and shot him down.

Men who fought in that battle praise Davis' courage, but some say that this mature, seasoned, pilot was also afflicted with a touch of the 'MiG madness' which affected so many Sabre jocks. At the same time, the lives of bomber crewmen were clearly at stake, and few of Davis' buddies doubt that had he survived, he would have stayed on top as the leading ace.

With Davis' loss, the USAF was deprived of one of its fine tacticians, and a future leader. Davis posthumously became the only Sabre pilot awarded the Medal of Honor in Korea. He was one of two F-86 pilots lost during the month, in return for a total of 17 MiGs destroyed. One of these kills, which was scored on 17 February, resulted in 335th FIS CO,

The USAF's very latest dedicated nightfighter – the F-94B – had been in-theatre from mid-1951, but it had still to claim a kill by the time the second Starfire unit arrived at Suwon. This jet was part of the second force sent to war, and wears the blue tip tank and tail stripes of the 319th FIS, originally from Moses Lake AFB, Washington. The Starfire did eventually go on to destroy four MiG-15s at night, but proved to be too fast to deal effectively with the Po-2/Yak-18 nuisance raiders *(Haller)*

On 1 April 1952, Maj William H Wescott of the of the 25th FIS/51st FIW, downed two MiGs, hence the gesture! He duly became the 12th US ace soon afterward on 26 April 1952. Wescott flew an F-86E-10-NA (51-2746) which he had named *LADY FRANCES*, and the crew chief had dubbed *MICHIGAN CENTER*. His was also the aircraft in which Col Gabreski scored his fifth kill *(USAF)*

Maj Zane S Amell, doubling his score, although he later became the second F-86 pilot lost in action that month. He too has been said to have been touched by 'MiG fever'.

A different kind of combat outfit, the 319th FIS, came to Suwon on 1 March 1952 as the second user of the F-94B nightfighter to enter the war. The 319th was to give new meaning to the concept of 'limited' warfare, with both pilots and radar operators (ROs) – well-trained and highly motivated – felling that they were being sent into battle with their hands tied behind their backs. The USAF was so concerned that it might lose an F-94B, together with its secret air-intercept radar, which would be of great interest to the Soviets, that the squadron was confined to flying south of the bomb line, except for the occasional dash north.

In the air-to-air fighting, March 1952 saw the Air Force's F-86 pilots chalk up 39 MiG kills, while sustaining just three losses. On 20 March 1952, the SAAF's No 2 Sqn – the 'Flying Cheetahs' – had its second brush with MiGs when a flight of four Mustangs was attacked by five MiG-15s. Lt Taylor's aircraft was hit and he was forced to bail out, but one of the MiGs was struck in the starboard wing by a long burst fired by Lt Enslin, and it broke off the engagement and headed back north.

Two Meteor F.8s (A77-920, A77-120) were lost to flak by No 77 Sqn during March whilst carrying out ground attack missions. However, the Aussies were also now becoming more frequent targets for aggressive MiG attacks, whose tactics appeared to have changed as they now ranged farther south to attack the RAAF jets. Australian pilots had scored just a solitary MiG kill up to this point.

Double scores were toted up on 1 April 1952 when Capt Iven C Kincheloe and Maj William H Wescott – both members of the of the 25th FIS/51st FIW – shot down two MiGs each. The number of F-86 aces was steadily rising. New aces included Bill Whisner, CO of the 51st FIW's 25th FIS, who became the seventh jet ace, and his wing's first, on 23 February, whilst Col Francis S Gabreski became the eighth (1 April), Capt Robert H Moore the ninth (3 April), Capt Kincheloe the tenth (6 April), Capt Robert J Love the eleventh (21 April) and Maj Wescott the war's twelfth (on 26 April).

Col Gabreski – then and today America's top living ace – got his fifth kill in an F-86E (51-2746) belonging to the 25th FIS/51st FIW which Bill Wescott had named *LADY FRANCES*, and the crew chief had dubbed *MICHIGAN CENTER* (the nickname assigned by a pilot appeared on the left nose whilst that assigned by crew chief and armourer appeared on the right nose, which meant that some jets had three names). Wescott got his fifth kill in the same aeroplane. The strapping Capt Iven C Kincheloe, who was six-foot-two, with silver-blond hair and the build of a football linebacker, became the first ace to get all of his kills while flying the same jet (51-2731), kept flyable by crew chief Dan Walker.

In April 1952 the scoreboard for the air-to-air combat along the Yalu River was 44 MiGs to four F-86s. The first attempt by the other side to

station aircraft south of the Yalu was countered on 22 April 1952 when Maj Elmer W Harris and Capt Kincheloe shot up the base at Sinuiju, destroying two Yak-9 fighters and possibly damaging a MiG-15. In Korea, enemy aircraft destroyed on the ground were not counted as kills, but the loss mattered to the enemy, nonetheless.

At several intervals during the war pilots crossed the forbidden Yalu to engage MiGs on their on turf, ignoring rules, politics and direct orders to stay out of Chinese air space. There were accidental crossings, whilst at times pilots decided on their own to jump the border deliberately. But for short periods at least this trans-border fighting involved more than just one pilot on a regular basis.

In the Suwon-based 51st FIW, Col Gabreski, Lt Col George Jones, Col Walker 'Bud' Mahurin, Maj William Whisner and others adopted a 'hot pursuit' policy, flying what they called 'Maple Special' incursions into Manchuria after purposely setting up situations which gave them a shot at fleeing MiG-15 pilots. These border crossings were kept secret from others at Suwon. Capt Kincheloe found out about 'Maple Special' by accident, and was inducted into the closed fraternity of participants.

Trips across the Yalu were an invitation to trouble. For example, 1st Lt Bill Ginther came back from a mission with revealing gun-camera film after he'd attacked a MiG-15 over Manchuria. Struggling to get away, the enemy pilot had dived to earth, pulling out just in time to pass along the runway at the crowded Antung airfield. Ginther's gun camera film, as Mahurin later described it, showed 'row after row of MiGs lined up on either side of the runway', so that 'it appeared that the F-86 was flying even below the tops of the MiG tails'. While enemy technicians stood on the MiGs watching, Ginther shot down his foe and somehow got away unscathed. Upon returning to base he burned his film straight after its one and only private showing.

1st Lt Joe Cannon, who flew F-86E Sabres with the 25th FIS, remembers what it was like to fight the MiG in the following passage.

'Of the 91 missions I flew, most of them were with "Kinch" (Capt Kincheloe) and "Gabby" (Col Gabreski, 51st FIW commander). On 2 April, "Kinch" and I entered the area near Sinanju, not far from the Yalu River, at about 48,000 ft. We dropped our external tanks when we spotted three flights of MiGs 5000 ft below us. We were lucky in that we were not pulling any contrails and they had not seen us. We rolled over and dove down on them. "Kinch" bagged one as we busted through the middle of the whole damned formation – not the smartest thing we ever did. I came so close to colliding with a MiG that

HONEST JOHN was the F-86E-10 Sabre (51-2747) flown by World War 2 ace, Col Walker 'Bud' Mahurin, who flew with the 51st FIW before transferring to command the 4th FIG, where he flew this aircraft. The Sabre also has the nickname *Stud* painted under its gun ports. Mahurin claimed that the large yellow stripes bordered in black were designed to set the 51st apart from the 4th (though the latter adopted them), and to increase morale. He was awarded aerial victories for 3.5 MiG-15s, scored on 6 January, 17 February and 5 March 1952 (1.5). He was shot down and captured on 13 May 1952 whilst flying another different Sabre. During his internment as a PoW, Mahurin was forced to sign 'confessions' drummed up by his captors, which he recanted when released after the armistice *(via Norman Taylor)*

An informal gathering of 25th FIS pilots, and the wing flight surgeon, Maj Bernard Brungardt (second from left). Others in this shot are, far left, Lt Harry Shumate, far right, ace Capt Iven Kincheloe, Jr, and second from right, Lt Joe Cannon *(Dr San Brungardt)*

as I went by, I looked the pilot straight in the face and I noticed that the he had a cloth helmet on! "Kinch" called out over the radio that it was my turn now (we alternated flying wing for each other). I pulled up hard and rolled. Going around I saw the jet I had just missed colliding with. He was heading for the Yalu, so I "split-S'ed" and came down behind him. After a three-second burst he began to burn.

'At about that moment, "Kinch" yelled, "Break left!". When I broke hard and turned my head to see who was on my tail, the entire world lit up. This MiG jockey proceeded to shoot the oxygen mask right off my face, blowing the canopy away, making my left wing half the size of my right one and shredding my rudder. When I punched out over the coast, several hundred miles from where I wanted to be, the MiGs set up a gunnery pattern on me coming down in the chute. "Kinch" was right in the middle of them, breaking their concentration up. MiGs were coming from everywhere. Some of them came so close, they were swinging me horizontally in the chute, but I swear that "Kinch" was behind every one that came by. What a sight! I was soon picked up by the Navy and returned to Suwon for dinner.'

SEA FURY MISSION

In the spring of 1952, the aircraft carrier HMS *Ocean* reached Korea with No 802 Sqn, equipped with Hawker Sea Fury FB.Mk 11s, embarked. Commonwealth aircraft carriers like *Ocean* operated on the west coast of Korea in the Yellow Sea, separated by the peninsula from US Navy vessels in the Sea of Japan. Sea Fury pilots regularly ran the expected gauntlet of withering gunfire to attack ground targets. One of them, Cdr Peter 'Hoagy' Carmichael, later remembered, 'Our biggest worry was flak. It kept you worried the whole time. Some of it was radar-controlled, and some used tracer. AA guns from 12.7 to 88 mm calibre were encountered, along with massed rifle and small-arms fire. Most AA weapons were very well concealed, sometimes in house in the villages, and sometimes with optical height finders, predictors and even radar. False targets were used as flak traps, and their fire discipline was excellent'.

A double kill was added to the victory roster on 3 May when Maj Donald E Adams (16th FIS/51st FIW) bagged a pair of MiG-15s. On 4 May, two Meteor F.8 pilots spotted nine MiGs flying farther south than usual, near Pyongyang. At low-level, where the RAAF pilots could negate the MiG's performance advantage, Plt Off J Surman racked up a 'probable' with two bursts of cannon fire – the starboard tailplane was shot of

Royal Navy Sea Fury FB.Mk 11s performed sterling work in the demanding ground attack role throughout the Korean conflict, with many of the aircraft themselves serving on consecutive carrier deployments as squadrons rotated machinery from out going to incoming carrier decks. A perfect example of this practice is seen here, as this No 802 Sqn machine still wears the ex-*Glory* 'R' code on its fin, although it is being manhandled into position for its next launch aboard HMS *Ocean* – the latter's code was 'O'
(Royal Navy)

A77-643 was on strength with No 77 Sqn when Plt Off Bill Simmonds scored his MiG kill in early May 1952. Indeed, the jet had only arrived fresh from the UK the month before. Here, it is seen taxing out over the pierced steel matting armed with eight HVARs – the F.8 is also wearing the OC's pennant beneath the cockpit. A77-643 was eventually shot down during a ground attack sortie in April 1953, having spent a full year on the combat roster at Kimpo
(No 77 Sqn via Tony Fairbairn)

the MiG and its jet exhaust exploded, but unfortunately it was not seen to crash. Four days later Plt Off Bill Simmonds fired on a MiG whilst flying A77-385, the enemy jet duly going into a spin and its pilot bailing out. Simmonds later said that he had 'fully exploited the F-8's virtues' in this combat by breaking hard into the MiG when his formation, 'Godfey Red', had been bounced. His max-G turn had forced the enemy to over-shoot, after which he reversed his evasive manoeuvre and latched onto the MiG's tail. Simmonds then passed over his quarry so closely that he could see the Chinese pilot in full detail.

That same day, Sabres made two rare kills of prop-driven fighters when 1st Lt James A McCulley and Capt Richard H Schoeneman (both from the 16th FIS/51st FIW) shot down a Yak-3 and an Il-10 respectively. Schoeneman was eventually credited with two MiG-15s as well, including a pair of half credits, for a total of three aerial victories.

On 13 May, an important USAF leader was lost when Col 'Bud' Mahurin was shot down and captured. Mahurin, who'd transferred to Kimpo to command the 4th FIG under the 4th FIW's Harry Thyng, was shot down by AAA on a bombing mission – he was not flying his own jet, nicknamed *HONEST JOHN* (F-86E-10 51-2747) during this sortie. His loss marred the continuing, but thus far premature, effort to transform the jet into a fighter-bomber by slinging two 1000-lb bombs beneath its inboard pylons. Later attempts were more successful.

On 26 May, a group of Skyknight pilots and support people, headed by Col Peter D Lambrecht, arrived at Kunsan, Korea. Within weeks, 14 F3D-2s, re-painted flat black with red lettering, had joined VMF(N)-513.

Soon after an officer who flew the F-86 regularly, Lt Gen Glen O Barcus became commander of the Fifth Air Force on 30 May, reporting to FEAF chief Lt Gen Otto P Weyland. In the air-to-air conflict, May brought 27 MiG kills in exchange for losses of five Sabres. Four more men became aces: Capt Robert T Latshaw became the 13th ace and Maj Donald E Adams the 14th (both on 3 May), Lt James H Kasler the 15th (15 May) and the soon-to-depart 4th FIW commander Col Thyng the 16th (20 May). The latter was already an ace from a previous war and could have gotten more MiGs, as he was known for 'handing over' opportunities to 'bag' a kill to younger pilots who flew on his wing. However, Harry Thyng had no need to prove anything to anybody.

On 8 May 1952 Capt Richard H Schoeneman of the 16th FIS registered a unique kill in an F-86 when he destroyed a North Korean Il-10 in MiG Alley *(via Jerry Scutts)*

In mid-1952 the first fighter-bomber missions flown by Sabres were performed. Here, two 500 lb bombs are positioned beneath an F-86E from the 25th FIS. *(via Jerry Scutts)*

Colour Plates

This 17-page section profiles many of the aircraft flown by the 39 UN aces of the Korean War, plus examples of unique fighters and bombers that enjoyed one-off successes against communist forces. A solitary MiG-15 profile is also included, a first for any volume on the Korean conflict. The artworks have all been specially commissioned for this volume, and profile artists Chris Davey and John Weal, plus figure artist Mike Chappell, have gone to great pains to illustrate the aircraft and their pilots as accurately as possible, following much in-depth research from original sources.

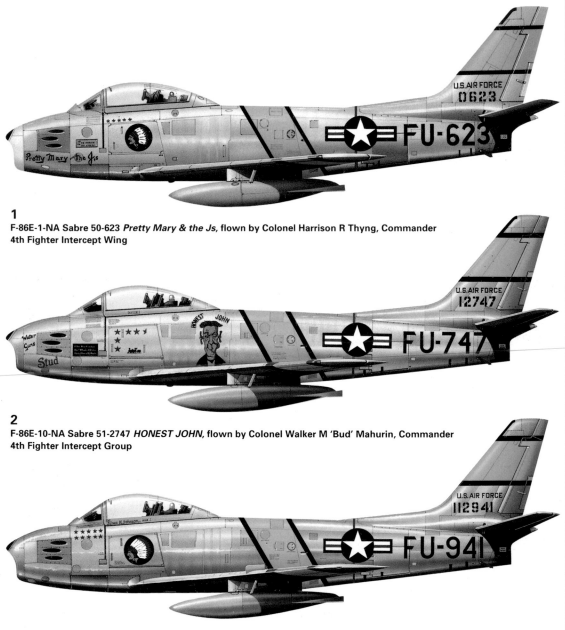

1
F-86E-1-NA Sabre 50-623 *Pretty Mary & the Js,* flown by Colonel Harrison R Thyng, Commander 4th Fighter Intercept Wing

2
F-86E-10-NA Sabre 51-2747 *HONEST JOHN,* flown by Colonel Walker M 'Bud' Mahurin, Commander 4th Fighter Intercept Group

3
F-86F-10-NA Sabre 51-12941, flown by Colonel James K Johnson, Commander 4th Fighter Intercept Wing

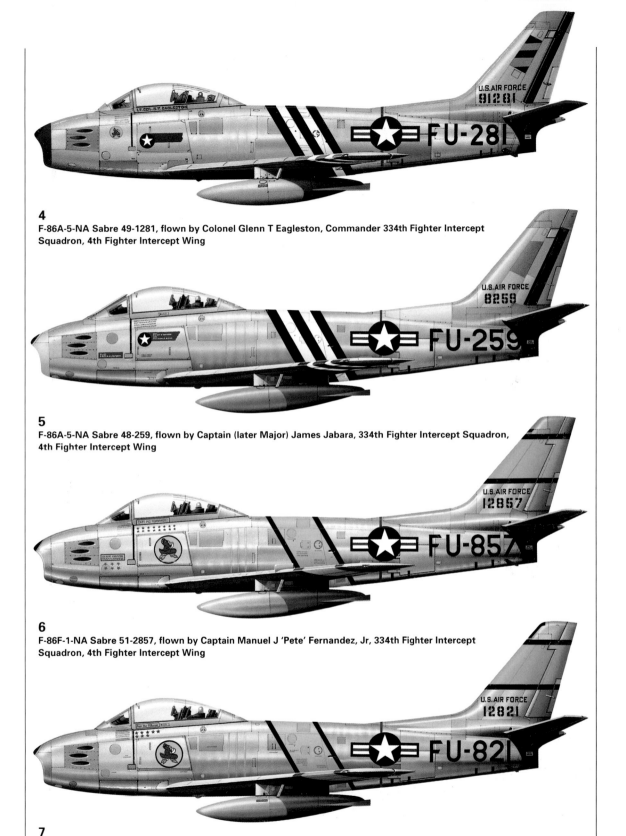

4
F-86A-5-NA Sabre 49-1281, flown by Colonel Glenn T Eagleston, Commander 334th Fighter Intercept Squadron, 4th Fighter Intercept Wing

5
F-86A-5-NA Sabre 48-259, flown by Captain (later Major) James Jabara, 334th Fighter Intercept Squadron, 4th Fighter Intercept Wing

6
F-86F-1-NA Sabre 51-2857, flown by Captain Manuel J 'Pete' Fernandez, Jr, 334th Fighter Intercept Squadron, 4th Fighter Intercept Wing

7
F-86E-10-NA Sabre 51-2821 flown by Major Frederick C 'Boots' Blesse, 334th Fighter Intercept Squadron, 4th Fighter Intercept Wing

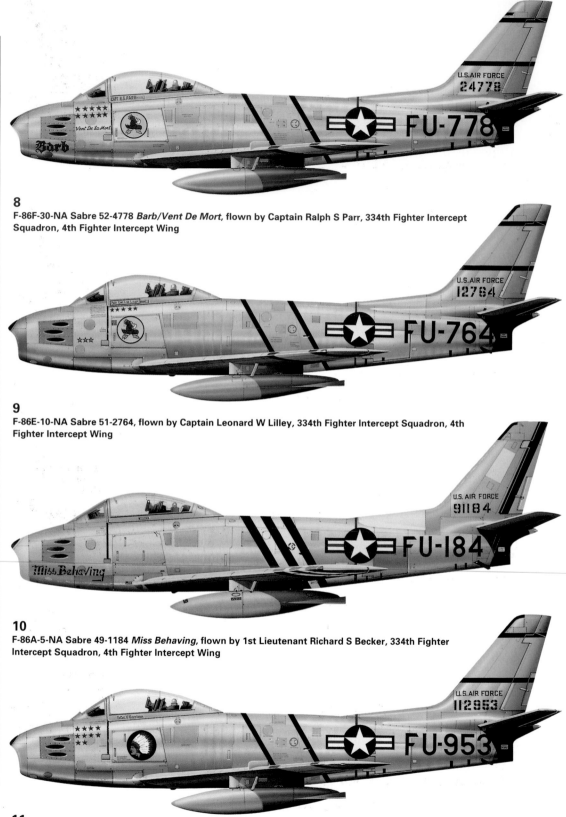

8
F-86F-30-NA Sabre 52-4778 *Barb/Vent De Mort*, flown by Captain Ralph S Parr, 334th Fighter Intercept Squadron, 4th Fighter Intercept Wing

9
F-86E-10-NA Sabre 51-2764, flown by Captain Leonard W Lilley, 334th Fighter Intercept Squadron, 4th Fighter Intercept Wing

10
F-86A-5-NA Sabre 49-1184 *Miss Behaving*, flown by 1st Lieutenant Richard S Becker, 334th Fighter Intercept Squadron, 4th Fighter Intercept Wing

11
F-86F-10-NA Sabre 51-12953, flown by Lieutenant Colonel Vermont Garrison, Commanding Officer 335th Fighter Intercept Squadron, 4th Fighter Intercept Wing

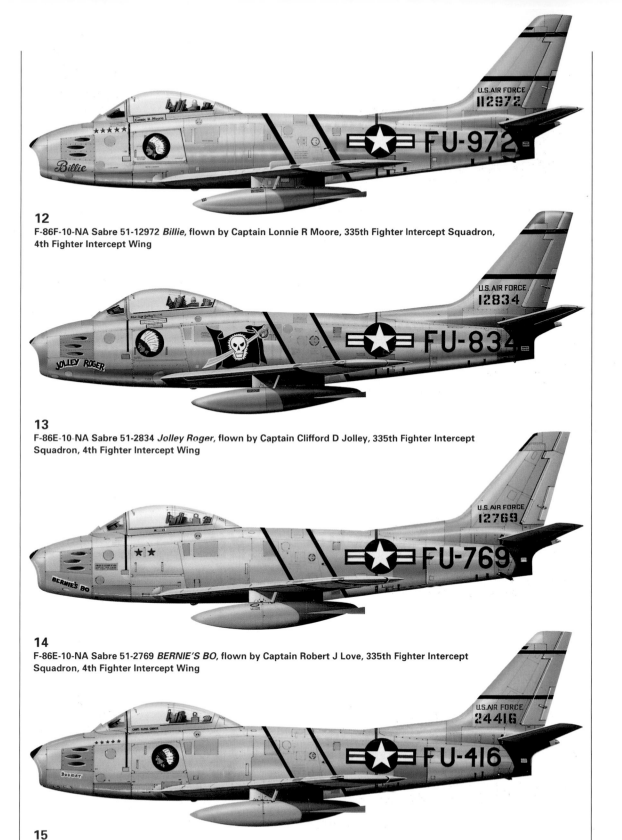

12
F-86F-10-NA Sabre 51-12972 *Billie*, flown by Captain Lonnie R Moore, 335th Fighter Intercept Squadron, 4th Fighter Intercept Wing

13
F-86E-10-NA Sabre 51-2834 *Jolley Roger*, flown by Captain Clifford D Jolley, 335th Fighter Intercept Squadron, 4th Fighter Intercept Wing

14
F-86E-10-NA Sabre 51-2769 *BERNIE'S BO*, flown by Captain Robert J Love, 335th Fighter Intercept Squadron, 4th Fighter Intercept Wing

15
F-86F-30-NA Sabre 52-4416 *Boomer*, flown by Captain Clyde A Curtin, 335th Fighter Intercept Squadron, 4th Fighter Intercept Wing

16
F-86A-5-NA Sabre 48-261, flown by Lieutenant Donald Torres, 335th Fighter Intercept Squadron, 4th Fighter Intercept Wing

17
F-86E-10-NA Sabre 51-2822 *THE KING/Angel Face & The Babes*, flown by Colonel Royal V 'The King' Baker, 336th Fighter Intercept Squadron, 4th Fighter Intercept Wing

18
F-86E-10-NA Sabre 51-2824 *Little Mike/Ohio Mike*, flown by Captain (later Major) Robinson Risner, 336th Fighter Intercept Squadron, 4th Fighter Intercept Wing

19
F-86A-5-NA Sabre 49-1225, flown by Major Richard D Creighton, 336th Fighter Intercept Squadron, 4th Fighter Intercept Wing

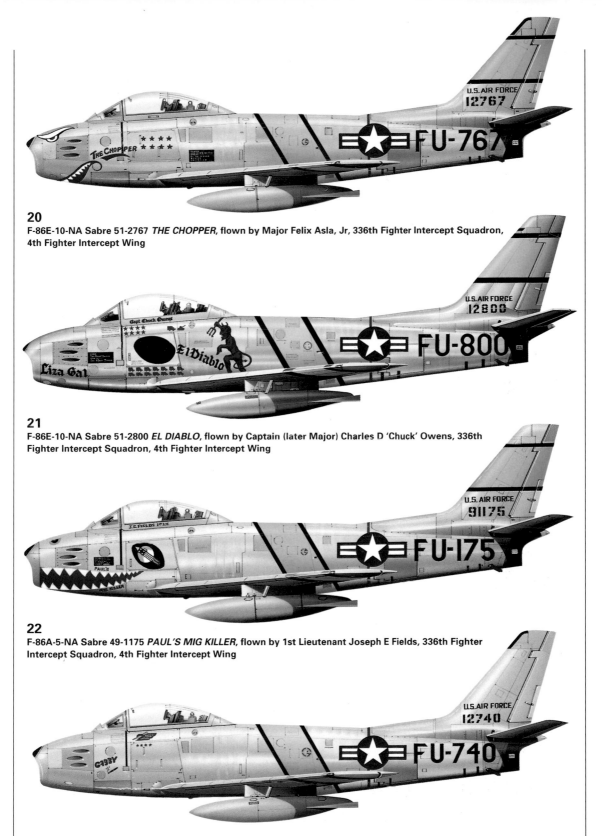

20
F-86E-10-NA Sabre 51-2767 *THE CHOPPER*, flown by Major Felix Asla, Jr, 336th Fighter Intercept Squadron, 4th Fighter Intercept Wing

21
F-86E-10-NA Sabre 51-2800 *EL DIABLO*, flown by Captain (later Major) Charles D 'Chuck' Owens, 336th Fighter Intercept Squadron, 4th Fighter Intercept Wing

22
F-86A-5-NA Sabre 49-1175 *PAUL'S MIG KILLER*, flown by 1st Lieutenant Joseph E Fields, 336th Fighter Intercept Squadron, 4th Fighter Intercept Wing

23
F-86E-10-NA Sabre 51-2740 *GABBY*, flown by Colonel Francis S Gabreski, Commander 51st Fighter Intercept Wing

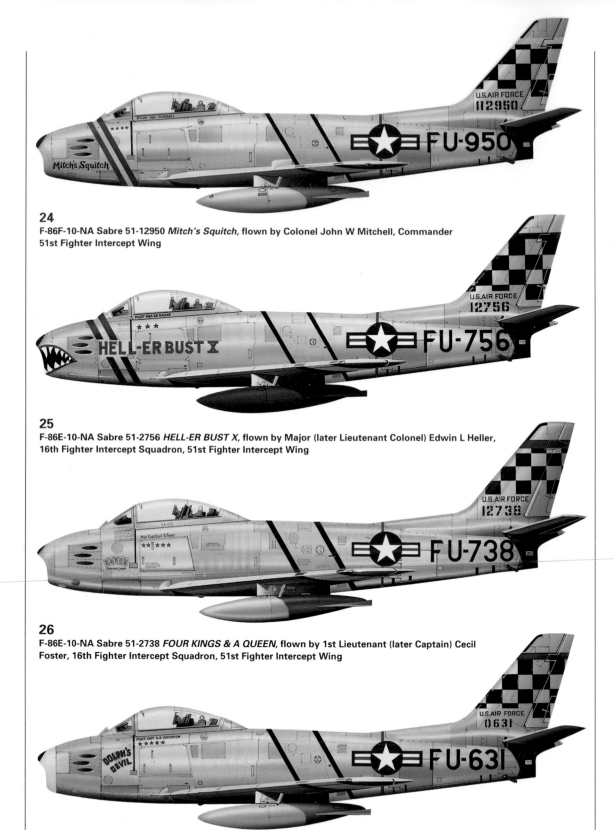

24
F-86F-10-NA Sabre 51-12950 *Mitch's Squitch*, flown by Colonel John W Mitchell, Commander 51st Fighter Intercept Wing

25
F-86E-10-NA Sabre 51-2756 *HELL-ER BUST X*, flown by Major (later Lieutenant Colonel) Edwin L Heller, 16th Fighter Intercept Squadron, 51st Fighter Intercept Wing

26
F-86E-10-NA Sabre 51-2738 *FOUR KINGS & A QUEEN*, flown by 1st Lieutenant (later Captain) Cecil Foster, 16th Fighter Intercept Squadron, 51st Fighter Intercept Wing

27
F-86E-1-NA Sabre 50-631 *DOLPH'S DEVIL*, flown by Captain Dolphin D Overton, 16th Fighter Intercept Squadron, 51st Fighter Intercept Wing

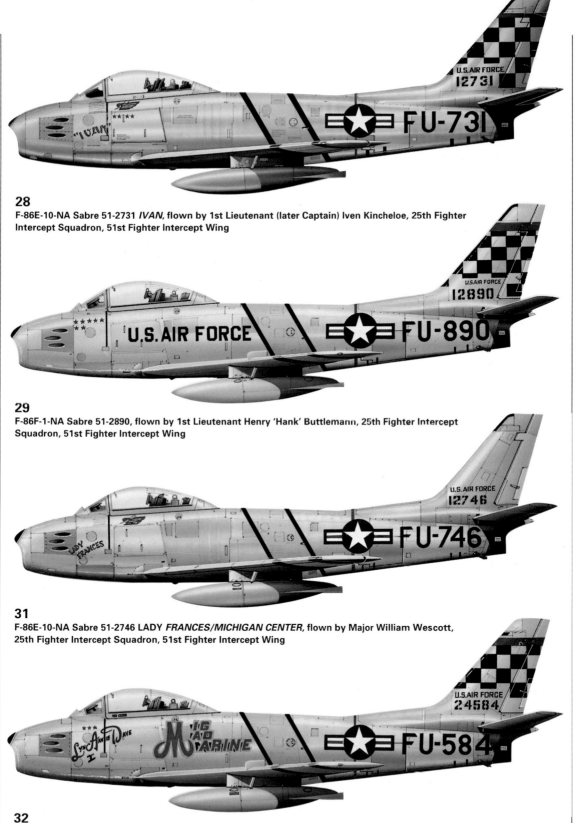

28
F-86E-10-NA Sabre 51-2731 *IVAN*, flown by 1st Lieutenant (later Captain) Iven Kincheloe, 25th Fighter Intercept Squadron, 51st Fighter Intercept Wing

29
F-86F-1-NA Sabre 51-2890, flown by 1st Lieutenant Henry 'Hank' Buttlemann, 25th Fighter Intercept Squadron, 51st Fighter Intercept Wing

31
F-86E-10-NA Sabre 51-2746 LADY *FRANCES/MICHIGAN CENTER*, flown by Major William Wescott, 25th Fighter Intercept Squadron, 51st Fighter Intercept Wing

32
F-86F-30-NA Sabre 52-4584 *MIG MAD MARINE/LYN ANNIE DAVE I*, flown by Major John Glenn, USMC, 25th Fighter Intercept Squadron, 51st Fighter Intercept Wing

30
F-86E-10-NA Sabre 51-2735 *Elenore E*, flown by Major William T Whisner, 25th Fighter Intercept Squadron, 51st Fighter Intercept Wing

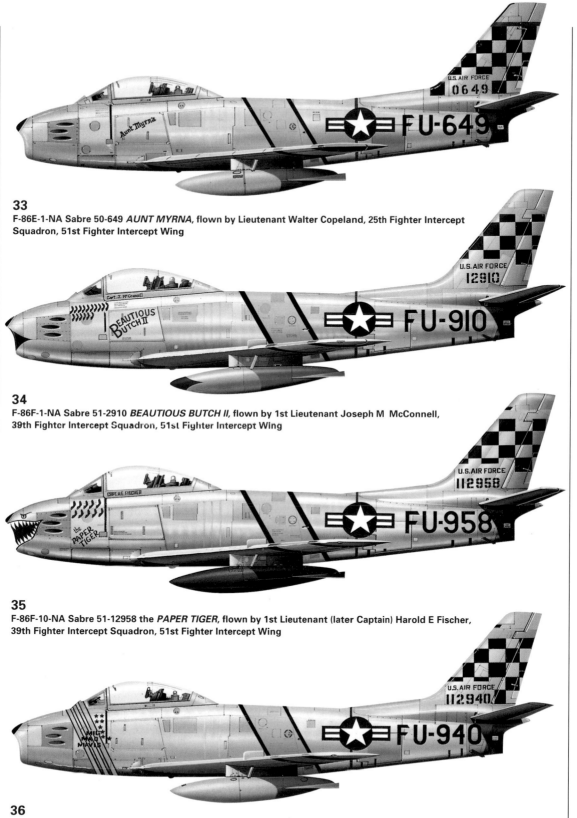

33
F-86E-1-NA Sabre 50-649 *AUNT MYRNA,* flown by Lieutenant Walter Copeland, 25th Fighter Intercept Squadron, 51st Fighter Intercept Wing

34
F-86F-1-NA Sabre 51-2910 *BEAUTIOUS BUTCH II,* flown by 1st Lieutenant Joseph M McConnell, 39th Fighter Intercept Squadron, 51st Fighter Intercept Wing

35
F-86F-10-NA Sabre 51-12958 the *PAPER TIGER,* flown by 1st Lieutenant (later Captain) Harold E Fischer, 39th Fighter Intercept Squadron, 51st Fighter Intercept Wing

36
F-86F-10-NA Sabre 51-12940 *MIG MAD MAVIS,* flown by Lieutenant Colonel George I Ruddell, Commanding Officer 39th Fighter Intercept Squadron, 51st Fighter Intercept Wing

37
F-86F-1-NA Sabre 51-2852 *DARLING DOTTIE*, flown by Major John F Bolt, USMC, 39th Fighter Intercept Squadron, 51st Fighter Intercept Wing

38
F-86F-1-NA Sabre 51-2897 *THE HUFF*, flown by Lt James L Thompson, 39th Fighter Intercept Squadron, 51st Fighter Intercept Wing

39
F-82G-NA Twin Mustang 46-383, flown by Lieutenant William 'Skeeter' Hudson, with Lieutenant Carl Fraser, 68th Fighter (All Weather) Squadron

40
F-94B-5-LO 51-5449, flown by Captain Ben Fithian, with Lieutenant Sam R Lyons, 319th Fighter Intercept Squadron

41
F-51D-30-NT Mustang 45-11736, flown by Lieutenant James Glessner, 12th Fighter Bomber Squadron,
18th Fighter Bomber Group

42
F-51D-30-NA Mustang 44-75728, flown by Major Arnold 'Moon' Mullins, 67th Fighter Bomber Squadron,
18th Fighter Bomber Group

43
F-86F-30-NA Sabre 52-4341 *MIG POISON*, flown by Major James P Hagerstrom, 67th Fighter Bomber
Squadron, 18th Fighter Bomber Group

44
F-84E-25-RE Thunderjet 51-493, flown by Lieutenant Jacob Kratt, Jr, 523rd Fighter Escort Squadron, 27th Fighter
Escort Wing

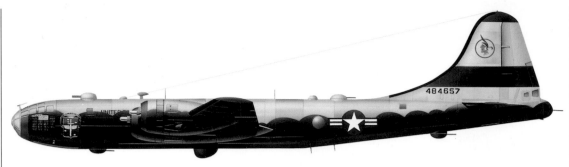

45
B-29B-60-BA Superfortress 44-84057 *COMMAND DECISION*, 28th Bomb Squadron,
19th Bomb Group (Medium), Kadena, Okinawa

46
F4U-5N Corsair (BuNo 24453) *ANNIE MO*, flown by Lieutenant Guy 'Lucky Pierre' Bordelon,
'Detachment Dog', VC-3, detached ashore to K-6 from USS Princeton

47
F9F-2 Panther (BuNo unknown), flown by Lieutenant Leonard Plog, VF-51, USS Valley Forge

48
F9F-2 Panther (BuNo unknown), flown by Lieutenant(jg) J D Middleton, VF-781, USS Oriskany

49
FG-1D (F4U-4) Corsair (BuNo 92701), flown by Captain Jesse Folmar, VMA-312

50
F4U-5N Corsair (BuNo 123180), flown by Captain John Andre, VMF(N)-513

51
F7F-3N Tigercat (BuNo unknown), flown by Captain E B Long with WO R C Buckingham, VMF(N)-513

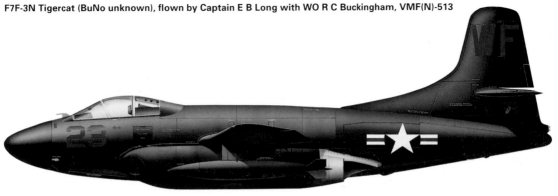

52
F3D-2 Skyknight (BuNo unknown), flown by Major William Stratton with M/Sgt Hans Haglind, VMF(N)-513

53
Sea Fury FB.Mk 11, flown by Lieutenant Peter 'Hoagy' Carmichael, No 802 Squadron, Fleet Air Arm, HMS *Ocean*

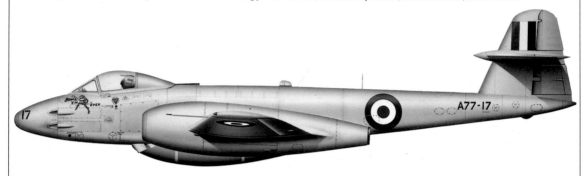

54
Gloster Meteor F .Mk 8 A77-17 *BOWL 'EM OVER!*, flown by Flying Officer Bruce Gogerly, No 77 Squadron, RAAF

55
Gloster Meteor F.MK 8 A77-851 *"HALESTORM"*, flown by Sergeant George Hale, No 77 Squadron RAAF

56
MiG-15 925, flown by Colonel Yevgeni Pepelyaev, commander of the 196th Istrebeitel Aviatsionnaya Polk
(Fighter Aviation Regiment)

1. A 1st Lieutenant of the 25th FIS/51st FIW at Suwon in the early summer of 1952

2. Captain Manuel 'Pete' Fernandez of the 334th FIS/4th FIW in the spring of 1953

3. Captain Harold 'Hal' Fischer of the 39th FIS/51st FIW at Suwon in late 1952

4. Lone USMC ace of the war, Major John F Bolt of the 39th FIS/51st FIW in June 1953

5. Colonel Yevgeni Pepelyaev, commander of the 196th Istrebeitel Aviatsionnaya Polk, late 1951

6. Sea Fury MiG killer Lieutenant Peter 'Hoagy' Carmichael of No 802 Sqn, embarked aboard HMS Ocean, in mid-1952

SUPERIOR SABRE

ol John W Mitchell took command of the 51st FIW on 13 June 1952, replacing Gabreski. Mitchell was the 11-kill World War 2 ace who had commanded the P-38G Lightning-equipped 339th FS, and had led the 18 April 1943 fighter mission which killed Japanese Admiral Isoru Yamamoto. In Korea, Mitchell was destined to add four MiG-15s to his tally, making him a triple ace.

The hard wing on late F-86Fs (replacing the leading-edge slats found on previous Sabres, including early F-86Fs), when combined with the all-flying tail, gave the Sabre both unmatchable manoeuvrability and the chance to better the MiG-15's previously untouchable service ceiling. Steps were taken to retrofit all F-86Fs with the new solid wing. The new wing was also known as the 'G-3' wing because it replaced the leading-edge slats with a smooth, unbroken, leading surface that was extended six inches at the wing root and three inches at the wing tip. To improve the flow of air over this redesigned wing, a six-inch barrier fence was added at the 70-per cent mark on the span.

For the first time the Sabre now had the performance to outfight the MiG-15 in every regime. The hard-wing F-86F could operate at 52,000 ft, had an improved climb rate, tighter turning circle and could achieve a speed in level flight that was at least ten knots faster than the F-86E.

The 4th Wing's 2nd Lt James F Low became the 17th, and most junior, American air ace with his fifth MiG kill on 15 June. Not as young as his rank suggested (he'd been an enlisted sailor in World War 2), 'Dad' Low was just six months out of flight school. He turned inexperience to his advantage – unlike older pilots, who had to change with the advent of new technologies, Low had no trouble learning how to use the A-4 automatic ranging gun sight on the F-86E and later Sabres.

'Dad' Low later appeared as the fictional character Pell in fellow Sabre pilot James Horowitz's novel, *The Hunters*, written under the pseudonym James Salter. The novel's 'bad guy', Pell is a defiant, risk-taking, junior fighter jock, later portrayed by Robert Wagner in the film of the book. Both Low and Horowitz (who later changed his name to Salter) acknowledge that storybook figure 'Pell' is, in fact, James F Low.

North Korean prop-driven fighters made another brief appearance on 20 June 1952 when 4th FIW Sabre pilots Col Royal N Baker, Capt Frederick C 'Boots' Blesse and 1st Lt George J Woods each shot down a La-9.

The 39th FIS 'Cobras', the final Sabre squadron committed to the air-to-air campaign along the Yalu, began to receive the improved F-86F model in July 1952. F-86Fs retained the all-flying tail, which had markedly improved the jet's manoeuvrability against the MiG, but early

This portrait of a busy, sandbag-guarded, Suwon flightline was snapped by ace, 1st Lt Hank Buttelmann, and it shows virtually all of the 25th FIS's F-86Es being readied for a patrol. In the foreground is the unit commander's jet, clearly denoted by the two nose stripes just aft of the gun ports – he can, in fact, be seen signing for the F-86 at the wing root, his crew chief looking on over the 'half colonel's' shoulder *(Henry Buttelmann)*

Capt James Horowitz, West Point class of 1945, shot down a MiG-15 on 4 July 1952 while flying an F-86E with the 335th FIS/4th FIW. He also used a typewriter equally as effectively as his Sabre. Under the pen name James Salter, he published a novel, *The Hunters*, about Sabre pilots fighting in Korea *(Martin Bambrick)*

Aces and wingmen: 335th FIS/4th FIW pilots (left to right), James Horowitz (one MiG-15); James F 'Dad' Low (nine MiG-15s); Al Smiley; Coy Austin (two MiG-15s) and a cigar-chewing Phil 'Casey' Colman (four MiG-15s, plus five kills in World War 2) *(Martin J Bambrick)*

Capt Clifford D Jolley, the 18th US ace of the war, eventually accounted for seven MiGs. Here, he holds a helmet bearing a death's head, painted for him by squadron mate Karl Dittmer, who also applied the nose art for a trio of F-86s *(Karl Dittmer)*

A victorious Lt Peter 'Hoagy' Carmichael of No 802 Sqn returns to HMS *Ocean* after his historic sortie on 9 August 1952. He later acknowledged that he was lucky to prevail over the poorly flown MiG-15

examples also retained leading-edge slats. The F-86 was to become superior to the MiG-15 in all respects only when the slatted wing was replaced with the '6-3' hard wing.

The 18th air ace, Capt Clifford D Jolley of the 335th FIS/4th FIW, got his fifth MiG on 8 August 1952 (after getting two kills in a single fight the previous day). The next day, Cdr Peter 'Hoagy' Carmichael of the Fleet Air Arm became the first British piston-engined pilot to shoot down a MiG-15. He was on a rail-wrecking mission between Manchon and Pyongyang when his wingman called out that MiGs were approaching. Carmichael turned his flight of four Sea Fury fighters in a scissors manoeuvre and saw two flights of four MiGs each swarming down on him. Almost immediately, Carmichael was on a collision course with a MiG-15. Both opened fire, but neither hit anything.

The Sea Furies spent several minutes tangling with the MiGs and at one point Carmichael spotted a jet pulling out in front of fellow Sea Fury pilot Flt Lt Brian 'Smoo' Ellis, an RAF exchange officer. 'The aircraft then proceeded northwards at a reduced speed with some of the other MiGs in company. Then two more MiGs came head-on towards me, but nothing happened until I saw another down below me, going very slowly, it seemed. I turned into him and fired and closed to 300 yards, firing all the time. The MiG looked a beautiful job. It just seemed to glide through the air. I lost sight of him momentarily. I turned and looked over my shoulder and saw an aircraft go into the deck and explode. For one horrible moment I thought it was one of my boys.'

A quick radio check revealed that all four Sea Furies were okay and that one MiG-15 was not. Its pilot had made the mistake of trying to dogfight with the slower, but highly manoeuvrable, Sea Furies. Carmichael's kill had been achieved in Sea Fury FB.Mk 11 WJ232, coded '114'.

HARD-WING SABRE

In August 1952 came the most important event since F-86 pilots began to wrest the advantage from their adversaries over MiG Alley. That month, Col Mitchell's 51st FIW flew its first missions with three F-86Fs with solid leading wing edges. The '6-3' hard wing jet was the final evolution of a design which had shown extraordinary promise (with the F-86A), had been developed to improve its manoeuvrability (F-86E), and had finally cancelled out the altitude advantage enjoyed by the MiG (with the slat-wing F-86F). Sabre pilots were still outnumbered, but no longer outgunned. In the '6-3' hard wing F-86F, they commanded the battlefield.

On 4 September, Maj 'Boots' Blesse shot down his fourth and fifth MiG-15s to become the 19th American ace. That day, vastly outnumbered Sabre pilots shot down 13 MiGs and sustained four losses in a hard-fought, protracted, duel. Six days later elements of the Corps' VMA-312 'Checkerboards', which were at sea aboard the escort carrier USS *Sicily* (CVE-118), came under MiG attack. Capts Jesse G Folmar and Walter E Daniels were bounced by eight MiG-15s, which made repeated firing runs on the slower F4U-4Bs as they tried to get out of the area. After one of the MiGs completed a run on the Corsairs, instead of breaking off to the side, the jet pulled up directly in front of Capt Folmar's guns. A quick burst of the 20 mm cannon set the MiG ablaze – the jet crashed minutes later. Another MiG retaliated with a burst of 37 mm fire which forced Capt Folmar to bail out, but he was rescued and returned to the ship. Capt Daniels was not hit and safely landed back aboard the carrier.

F-86 pilot Capt Robinson Risner (336th FIS) became the war's 20th US ace with his fourth and fifth kills on 21 September. He had flown fighters in Panama during World War 2, and then in the Oklahoma Air Guard. He had badgered his way to Korea by accepting a reconnaissance assignment, then turned on the charm to get himself shifted to F-86s. An official history by Gen T R Milton, intended as a tribute to Risner, unwittingly gives a new perspective on the Korean fighting.

'The F-86 Sabre was the vehicle in which the new aces of the jet age were achieving stardom, and MiG Alley was their stage. Even though the Korean War itself was viewed with distaste or apathy by an America largely unaffected by that conflict, the battles in MiG Alley had taken on the aura of an international sporting event. The race for top honours among Joe McConnell, Jim Jabara and Pete Fernandez was front page news; it overshadowed the exploits of World War 2 aces like Francis Gabreski, John Meyer and Robin Olds, who were proving that jet combat was not exclusively a kid's game. The battle for leading MiG killer also obscured the lesser-known aces, Risner among them.'

These insights have value, but illustrate the peril of 'lazy history'. There was indeed an 'ace race' among younger men, but not until months later, whilst Robin Olds got no closer to Korea than an F-86D unit in Pittsburgh! Still, the official history is illuminating, as Gen Milton continues.

'Risner's transfer to the 4th FIW was not without its rough moments, brought on by the intensely competitive game in MiG Alley. Risner had shown from the first day that he was cut out for aerial combat. Thus, when the new guy from the recce outfit began to score kills, he had to face a bit of jealousy on the part of some of his seniors. It was nothing serious, but reflected the atmosphere of the time. The F-86 pilots were the glamour boys of an otherwise unpopular war, and glamour is not easily shared, one exception to the rule being the day Pete Fernandez called out to Risner's flight that he had 30 MiGs cornered in case anyone wanted to help.

'At any rate, Risner, on his way to eight victories, had quickly proved he belonged in the air combat major leagues. His wildest day resulted in both a kill and one of the best war stories one is ever likely to hear.

'Risner and his wingman were flying escort for a fighter-bomber mission against a chemical plant at the mouth of the Yalu. A wide screening turn took their two F-86s over a Chinese airfield near Antung, and Risner was soon engaged with a MiG. The ensuing dogfight, from 30,000 ft to the deck, was the real-life equivalent to the climactic scene

Capt Robinson Risner (336th FIS) became the war's 20th US ace with his fourth and fifth kills on 21 September 1952. He was one of three Korean War aces who later became PoWs in North Vietnam – the others were James Kasler and James F Low. Now a retired brigadier general, Risner is widely regarded as one of the greatest of all USAF fighter pilots *(USAF)*

Sabres of the 4th FIW wearing the markings which were finally settled upon by late 1951 or early 1952. The yellow bands on fuselage and wings became standard for all F-86 operators, but the yellow band on the tail became the trademark of the 4th. The jet in the foreground is a very early F-86A-5-NA (48-195), and is one of the earliest Sabres to have been employed in combat in Korea – it was also one of the last A-models left on strength with wing *(USAF)*

On strength with the 336th FIS at the time Risner was with the unit, this spotless F-86E is unusually devoid of any personal markings, although it does proudly wear the distinctive 'Rocketeers' emblem below the cockpit *(Eugene Summerich via Jerry Scutts)*

in *Star Wars*. The MiG rolled, half-rolled, stalled, did inverted turns, with Risner all the while in pursuit, firing his guns every time it appeared in his pipper. Once, they ended up in close formation, wingtip to wingtip, staring at one another. The end seemed near when the MiG, leading a descending chase close to the speed of sound, half-rolled and began a "split-S" at 1500 ft. This appeared to be a suicidal manoeuvre, but the pilot pulled out along a dry river bed, blowing dust and small rocks in his wake. Once more the game was on as Risner, momentarily entranced by the acrobatic show, took up the chase.

'The MiG led them between the hangars of a Chinese airfield, then down the runway, Risner's wingman still hanging on and warning of heavy flak. Finally, the MiG crashed, taking with it the finest pilot Risner had ever seen. Then came the problem of getting home. The wingman's fuel tank had been hit and was losing fuel rapidly. There was no chance that he could make it back to base, but Cho-do island did have a rescue unit. Acting with what had to be supreme self-confidence, Risner told his wingman to shut down his engine and stand by for a push.

'Pushing a jet fighter with another jet fighter is not a manoeuvre pilots practice. In fact, it is doubtful anyone had ever tried it successfully before or since, but it worked that day. Despite the streaming hydraulic fluid that obscured his vision, Risner pushed the flamed-out F-86 towards Cho-do, where his wingman bailed out. Tragically, though the bailout was successful, the pilot drowned when the wind caught his chute.'

Something similar happened within days to 'Boots' Blesse who was temporarily the top ace then in the fray with eight MiG-15s and one La-9 to his credit. He ran out of fuel during a mission over MiG Alley, ejected over the Yellow Sea, and was rescued by an SA-16A Albatross amphibian.

ROCKET BOOST

In September 1952, in a misguided move, selected pilots of the 335th FIS/4th FIW at Kimpo were equipped with what one of them called 'our six secret weapons'. These were early F-86Fs modified with three internal rocket-boost motors, based upon JATO (jet-assisted take-off) bottles used to help heavily loaded warplanes get off the runway. The rockets could be fired simultaneously or in train.

As one of the pilots recalls, 'Three of these (rocket-boosted F-86Fs) had wing slats like our F-86As and Es, while the other three had hard leading-edges on the wings, which were to come with the most advanced F-86Fs.

'Capt Clifford Jolley decided we would use them in pairs with the same wing configuration rather than mixing them in a flight. Our tests also showed that the JATO was most effective when fired all at once.

'I flew three missions in the "F" in September and had mixed feelings about it. At altitude the bird would not hold stable, but would insist on gaining height for several seconds, then losing it. No matter how hard I tried, I could not stop the damned thing from doing this. We only flew them as a two-ship element, with a floating lead, and they always seemed

Fighter ace Jolley and faithful crew chief Sgt Ernie Balasz pose in front of 'their' F-86E-10-NA, which bears more examples of Karl Dittmer's artistic creativity. The latter accounted for two MiGs on 1 August and 9 September 1952, whilst all seven of Jolley's kills were scored on his single tour with the 335th FIS 'Chiefs' *(Cliff Jolley)*

to be out of phase with each other. In a hard turn, they reacted worse than a P-51 with a full aft-fuselage tank. I mean they tried to swap ends and it took considerable forward stick to break the inevitable stall.

'On the plus side, it sure was nice to have that extra 3000 lbs of thrust when you needed to close the gap between you and a MiG. And once the units were fired, the bird flew normally. I was flying one with Jolley shortly after he had his dunk in

F-86s of the 336th FIS 'Rocketeers' launch from Kimpo airfield for a combat sweep along MiG Alley. In the foreground is a North American F-86E-10-NA (51-2834, *UNCLE DOMINICK II*) and behind it a Canadair F-86E-6-CAN (52-2857), one of 60 fighters produced for the USAF in Canada. The E-model Sabre introduced an 'all-flying tail' which enhanced manoeuvrability and narrowed the gap in performance with the MiG-15. After the first year of the Korean War, the 4th FIW wore yellow bands on its Sabres, and was distinguished from other fighter wings by having the yellow band also emblazoned in the fin of its aircraft *(Sherman Tandvig)*

the Yellow Sea. Someone had reported MiGs well up-river from Antung. We got into the area, but didn't see anything until we both hit bingo fuel. Just as we turned toward Kimpo, I spotted a MiG going toward Antung on our side of the river. I called Jolley and headed for him. He mentioned our marginal fuel state, but I elected to attack anyway and closed to about 2000 ft, barely in range for our ".50s". I caught him with several bursts, but was hurrying my attack and ran out of ammo before I realised I was closing to effective range. I doubt that he made it to Antung, but we couldn't wait around to see.

'Capt Troy G Cope and I flew a mission in a couple of the rocket-equipped "secret weapons". We were headed toward Antung, about 50 miles out, when Cope got behind a MiG and opened fire. He fired his JATO and hosed off a few bursts, but I saw a couple of MiGs coming up behind him. They were almost within range, so I called, "Cope, you have a couple coming up behind. Call the break when you get tired of shooting at that guy". Then I got an urgent call back telling me to break left *now*.

'Hell, I was *already* to Cope's left. I made a hard break to the left and saw a MiG go past my right wing, close enough to reach out and touch. I turned back to hose him. "No! No!", came another warning call. I whipped back to the left as another MiG went by less than a hundred feet to my right. By then my bird was in a complete stall. I pushed forward hard on the stick, trying to break the stall, then glanced back at both MiGs as they tried to get into shooting position and found myself still stalling and falling. They gave up after about 270 degrees of my stalled turn. I climbed back up to altitude and the two of us headed more or less parallel to the river, toward the coast. Shortly, I saw a pair of MiGs followed by another pair crossing in front of us. I made a turn to attack, approaching at about a 30-degree angle to them. As we approached, I noticed that I was on a collision course with a third pair of MiGs! The leader was at my left and slightly high. If Cope was watching me he might not notice this pair. I called, "Cope, watch out for that other pair!"

'By then I was at a critical spot, and whipped my bird up and to the right in a half roll which put me directly over the lead MiG. That put him in a bad spot. I watched as he started to turn left, then right, then into a hard left turn. I rolled left and down. He crossed 200 ft in front of me and I considered hosing off a burst. I should have because I could have ripped him to shreds. As it was, he headed up and swung back toward the north. I knocked a few holes in his tail, then fired my JATO in an attempt to

Liza Gal/El Diablo was the F-86E-10-NA (51-2800) flown by Capt Charles D 'Chuck' Owens of the 336th FIS from Kimpo. During a hectic period in the Korean fighting, Owens was thought to have extracted a heavy penalty from the MiG-15 force on the far side of the Yalu – perhaps as many as the nine represented by kill symbols under the canopy of 51-2800. In fact, Owens, who was promoted to Major in mid-1952, was officially credited with just two MiG-15 kills on 30 April 1952 and 7 August 1952. This jet has had its 'Rocketeers' emblem painted over, hence the black swatch below the MiG kill markings
(via Norman Taylor)

VMF(N)-513 finally achieved success with their small force of Skynights on 2 June 1952 when Maj William Stratton, Jr, and MSgt Hans Hoglind destroyed a 'Yak-15' during a B-29 escort mission. This historic first jet versus jet night kill was soon celebrated on the side of their victorious Skynight *(Doug Rogers)*

catch him. While the JATO was on I called, "Cope, I've fired my weapon. Do you have me in sight?"

'No response. "Oh hell", I thought. "He's hit that other MiG". As I approached the area I noticed MiGs at different altitudes. All were milling around two smoke columns coming up from the forest below.

'I started to make a high-speed pass to see if I could identify the types of the crashed birds, but decided against it. I wish I had taken the chance, though it wouldn't have changed anything.' Capt Cope was lost in action and the experiment with the boosted Sabres came to an end.

In September 1952, Sabre pilots of the 4th and 51st FIWs were credited with 61 MiG kills and seven probable kills, while four Sabres were lost in air-to-air combat. Capt Jolley recalled that 'only four of us were selected to fly these aircraft because they demanded a little extra "feel". They were tail-heavy and started porpoising at 35,000 ft. I was able to catch the last two MiGs I destroyed with this gimmick, but without it I might have been just as successful; because of the heavy tail "mushout" I got on a split-S to initiate the attack'. The boost scheme was abandoned.

When Col Harrison R Thyng went home after his eleven-month tenure as commander of the 4th FIW on 2 October 1952, he was entitled to feel satisfied that he'd turned the tide against the MiG-15. An ace in two wars, and a leader willing to take risks to help his men, Thyng, as the premier American fighter wing commander of his era, has now been all but forgotten. Partly due to the colonel's efforts (the 4th enjoyed preference in pilot assignments over the 51st), the 4th wing in October 1952 was probably the finest fighter unit ever put into the field by any air arm. The press ignored Harry Thyng completely upon his return to the USA.

In the late months of 1952, an incredible 30 MiGs went down during dogfights without being fired at. Sabre pilots found themselves observing a series of abrupt, uncontrollable, spins from which the Chinese pilots were unable to recover. Whatever caused these spins, the MiG pilots got better at it. In early 1953, pilots observed 24 MiGs going into spins, and although five pilots ejected or died, the others recovered. No explanation has ever emerged for this 'temporary' problem with the MiG-15.

The 4th FIW was now commanded by Col James K Johnson and the 51st by Col John W Mitchell. The two F-86 groups were constantly challenged in their thrust-and-parry campaigning along MiG Alley.

Just after midnight on 2 November, a VMF(N)-513 F3D-2 Skyknight flown by Maj William T Stratton and radar operator MSgt Hans Hoglind made radar contact with a communist jet which they believed to be a straight-wing Yak-15, although this has never been confirmed. The crew lost the contact, then re-established it. Squinting into the night sky, Stratton spotted the orange glow of the 'Yak's' jet exhaust. He fired three short bursts of cannon fire. The first caught the Yak's left wing, the second and third its fuselage area, and the it went down in flames, leaving the Skyknight crew flying through a detritus of smoke and debris. This was the first kill at night using an air intercept radar in a jet. On 8 November,

Capt O R Davis scored the USMC's first confirmed jet-v-jet kill when his F3D-2 downed a MiG-15.

Col Royal N Baker, 4th Group commander, became the 21st US jet ace on 17 November 1952, and eventually claimed 12 MiGs and one La-9. Capt Leonard W 'Bill' Lilley of the 334th FIS/4th FIW got his fifth MiG on 18 November 1952 to become the 22nd ace, whilst another rare double score was toted up two days later when Capt Paul E Jones (39th FIS/51st FIW) got two MiGs in a single fight. On 22 November, Capt Cecil G Foster of the 51st became the 23rd ace.

Capt Karl Dittmer (335th FIS/4th FIW) was one of those pilots who didn't quite make ace status, his final score totalling three kills – a MiG-15 on 1 August 1952 and two more on 10 September. Dittmer was also the artist who painted the nicknames on his own *BETTY BOOPS*, on Marty Bambrick's *WHAM BAM*, on Troy Cope's *ROSIE* and on Hank Crescibene's *NEWARK FIREBALL*. In the following passages he describes what it was like to fly out of Kimpo and head for MiG Alley.

'We'd try to keep alert. The key was to spot the "bandits" when they came across the Yalu. Sometimes, we'd get help from our radar site on the island of Cho-do, callsign "Dentist". Sometimes they took us by surprise. If someone spotted MiGs and had time, they'd call to let other flights know their location and general heading. One day, two of us found about 50 MiGs in a big, loose, gaggle. We jumped into the middle of them. This may sound stupid, but being outnumbered gave us one very good advantage – I knew where my wingman was and he knew where I was, and we could shoot at everything else!

'I have no idea how many MiGs I hit, but got strikes on several. Finally, I noticed a MiG cross below and in front of me. I made a turn that aligned me for an attack, used the excess altitude to get into an excellent shooting position, then squeezed the trigger. Nothing happened. I was out of ammunition. I was also very angry. If it had been possible, I would have yanked out the control stick and beat the MiG pilot on the head with it. Instead, we went home. A few days later, I was pulling duty at the Mobile Control unit on the north end of Kimpo's air strip. From the chatter on our radio, it was obvious the troops had found MiGs. Shortly, flights were coming in with their noses blackened from firing their six .50 cal guns.

'Traffic had pretty well quit when I heard a pilot call, "Kimpo, I'm about 30 miles out at 15,000, flamed out".

'"Roger. We're landing toward the south."

'Three Marine Corsairs were taxying toward the runway. I pressed my mike button. "Kimpo

Col Royal N Baker's F-86E-10-NA (51-2822) was liberally adorned with appropriate artwork, the 4th FIG's CO flying this jet on several MiG killing sorties. The 21st US ace of the war, Baker had only had a single red star painted on the aircraft when this shot was taken in the late summer of 1952 *(via Jerry Scutts)*

Seen at the rear area maintenance base in Tsuiki, Japan, *FATHER DAN* is a F-86E-10-NA Sabre (51-2738), and it displays the Confederate battle flag and the blue-bordered red/white shark's 'dentures' of 'Tiger Flight', 25th FIS/51st FIW – three red stars can also be seen below the cockpit. This aircraft was assigned to Capt Cecil G Foster, who became the 23rd American fighter ace on 22 November 1952 – like most aces, Foster flew other Sabres whilst racking up his nine aerial victories. Note the removal of access panels, including the panel on the nose just forward of the windscreen, and the pierced steel planking that was in use throughout both Korea and Japan at the time *(via Norman Taylor)*

As in any conflict, the US Sabre force sustained about half of its aircraft losses in non-combat mishaps. This F-86E-1-NA Sabre (50-660), nicknamed *PEERLESS, INC.*, was flown by several 4th FIW MiG killers. However, it was a new pilot, 1st Lt John Ferebee, who took 50-660 aloft on 28 November 1952 and wrote it off upon returning to Kimpo *(USAF via John Ferebee)*

A selection of Karl Dittmer's chums at the 335th FIS pose for a photo in the autumn of 1952. They are (left to right); 2nd Lt Michael E DeArmond, who became a PoW after being shot down flying an F-86E nicknamed *ERIC'S REPLY*, which was usually flown by British exchange officer, William B Harbison; 1st Lt Billy B Dobbs who was credited with four MiGs, and was later killed in a T-33 crash; Maj Zane S Amell, 335th FIS CO, who claimed two MiGs; 1st Lt Boobie L Smith who got one MiG; Capt Philip E Colman, who got five kills in World War 2 and four in Korea; and 2nd Lt Coy L Austin who claimed two MiGs *(USAF)*

Tower, hold those F4Us short. We have an F-86 coming in flamed out". They continued on. I repeated my call. No luck. They went onto the runway, with the leader and Three on the left, Two on the right. I screamed at the tower "Get those damn Corsairs off the runway!" The leader added throttle, took his time checking both magnetos, then added power and accelerated down the runway. I continued to holler at the Corsairs to get the hell off.

'Once the leader was well down the runway, Number Two went through his mag check, released brakes, and headed down the runway. I was still fuming over the mike. Number Three was just finishing his mag check when the flamed-out F-86 swooshed by him and touched down. Three, as if nothing had happened, released his brakes and passed the F-86 on his take-off roll!

'Another day, when I was not scheduled to fly, a "light" colonel who commanded the Air Base Group flew my F-86E. His wingman was flying one of the few F-86A models in our squadron. The A model had a conventional flight control system, while all later birds had hydraulic-operated flight controls. The colonel spotted a MiG quite low, so he and his wingman made a very steep dive to attack. The colonel pulled out a bit too hard and blacked out briefly. Ain't no wonder, for the gauge that records Gs that have been applied to the aircraft leaves a needle at the highest reading and it indicated 11 Gs. The bird is supposed to break at more than nine, but is stronger than engineered. Anyway, the colonel loused up his attack due to blacking out. His wingman couldn't come out of the dive as he intended and he ended up well below the MiG, so he didn't do any good either. The overstress left small wrinkles on the fuselage, just above the wing's trailing edge. My bird was a bit faster after that!

'Another day Cliff Jolley got into a fight and with fuel way low, broke out and headed for home. However, he didn't get away unscathed. A MiG hosed his bird with one cannon shell, knocking off the left earpiece of his helmet. Jolley didn't have enough fuel to make it back, and had to eject over the Yellow Sea. He dropped the ruined helmet when approaching the water in order to see how close he was to it. Fortunately, the rescue helicopter picked him up okay.'

On the night of 10 December 1952 VMF(N)-513 registered another first. It involved one of the most experienced electronic 'wizards' in the Marines, and an air-to-air victory which required no visual contact. 1st Lt Joseph A Corvi was an F3D pilot who, when on the

ground, specialised in electronics for the squadron. He and his radar operator, Sgt Dan George, were flying in the Sinanju area when the latter picked up an enemy aircraft on his scope. It was too far away for visual contact, so the radar-controlled guns were locked onto the target and Corvi opened fire at what he saw on his radar.

'We did not know that we had made this kill', Corvi said later, 'until my R/O reported a wing and flaming debris flying past us'. Thus, Corvi was the first pilot to actually locate, lock on and fire by use of the new radar equipment. The enemy were flying a Po-2, a difficult aircraft to pick up because of its partial fabric and wood construction. That same night, Corvi and George were also credited with a probable kill as well.

By December the North Koreans had employed a second aircraft type to carry out their 'Bedcheck Charlie' nuisance raids – the Yak-18, which had been designed as a primary trainer. Though not as numerous as the Po-2, it still became a factor in the night fighting. Only slightly easier to track on radar than the Po-2, the Yak-18 (first flown in 1945) had a basic all-metal structure with mixed fabric and metal covering. A simple, machine, it offered an enclosed canopy for its tandem, two-man, crew, although they did not hesitate to 'open up' and toss out hand-held bombs when flying over tempting targets – it does not appear the Yak-18 had underwing shackles for ordnance. It was powered by a 160 hp M-11FR radial engine, and could drive nightfighter crews crazy with its top speed of 154 mph. With a combat radius of about 310 miles, the Yak-18 had slightly less endurance than the Po-2, but it was a threat nonetheless.

United Nations forces in Korea began 1953 confronting an air armada of 1485 aircraft, including 950 MiG-15s, 165 propeller-driven fighters, 100 Ilyushin Il-28 twin-jet bombers and 270 other types. Lt Gen Glen O Barcus, Fifth Air Force commander, was particularly concerned about the Il-28 bombers, two of which had made a provocative flyby along the Yalu. The bombers were seen this one and only time, never to reappear again.

Rugged up against the bitter Korean winter, an unidentified marine groundcrewman stands in front of 'his' immaculate VMF(N)-513 F3D Skynight at Kunsan in late 1952. The three radar sets fitted into the portly Douglas nightfighter made the jet rather maintenance-heavy for the dedicated engineering teams assigned to the unit – VMF(N)-513's nickname of the 'Flying Nightmares' was often truer for the home side than the enemy! *(USMC)*

SKYKNIGHT KILL

The F3D-2 Skyknight force in Korea had grown to 24 aircraft by early 1953 – now the Marines could provide serious help when they went north at night to escort B-29s. The corpulent Skyknight was designed as a shipboard nightfighter, though it never flew in action from carrier decks. The F3D-1 made its maiden flight in the postwar era (on 23 March 1948) and was powered by two 3000 lb thrust Westinghouse J34-WE-24 turbojet engines, mounted on the lower edges of the forward fuselage, beneath the roots of its straight wing. Pilot and radar observer sat side-by-side. The F3D-1 version when introduced in Korea had a gross weight of 26,850 lbs, making it underpowered even with twin engines, and was armed with four 20 mm cannon. The F3D-1 was credited with a maximum speed of 565 mph at 20,000 ft. The F3D-2 version introduced improvements in engine and air intercept radar, and although the type looked big and brutish, it was effective in its nocturnal role.

Maj Jack Dunn of VMF(N)-513 was flying one of the dull black Skyknights with radar operator MSgt Lawrence Fortin beside him on 12 January 1953 when they engaged MiG-15s near Sinanju. Dunn's recalls, 'It was pitch dark and we were right in the middle of it. The MiGs were all over the place. They attempted to lure us out and away from the

A more than familiar sight at Kunsan – an F3D-2 has its AN/APG-26 gun lock-on radar adjusted prior to the next sortie. VMF(N)-513 had 24 jets in-theatre by January 1953, and the maintenance effort involved in keeping them airworthy was a credit to the 'Corps. Facilities at Kunsan were basic, and the vagaries of the weather in the region played merry hell with the electrics in the Douglas jet *(James Goff)*

All the hard slog on the ground was more than worth it when a Skyknight crew inflicted damage on the enemy. On 12 January 1953 Maj Jack Dunn and MSgt Lawrence Fortin did just that when they destroyed a MiG-15 near Sinanju, the communist fighter being one of several that attempted to intercept a formation of B-29s heading into North Korea. Here, Maj Dunn is seen wearing his DFC, which was awarded after his aerial success *(USMC)*

bomber stream by flying right up to the edge of the formations and then turning quickly back towards the Yalu. We stayed right with the B-29 and they were able to bomb their targets at Sinanju with no mishaps.

'After the bombers headed back south, our F3Ds remained in the area, with our ground control vectoring us in various directions toward "bandit" activity. All of a sudden, this aircraft flew in front of us with his wing lights on. My radar operator had him on the screen and began giving me vectors to follow, while at the same time I was telling our ground control at Cho-do what we were seeing. They came back and said that there were no friendlies in the area and for us to go after him. It took the better part of five minutes to get a "lock-on", and as we were getting closer and closer it seemed strange that an F3D could close the gap on a much faster MiG. Because of this fact, I can only guess that the pilot was "dogging it" to enable me to stay close enough to follow, but still just out of shooting range. Cho-do ground control told me we were now directly over the earlier bomber target of Sinanju. The enemy fighter commenced circling to the left, with his wing lights still on.

'At that moment, about six searchlights from the ground switched on and caught us broadside. It was just like bright sunlight with an instant blinding effect. The AA)anti-aircraft fire) cut loose and bounced us around a bit, but we were fortunate to avoid any hits. I was able to keep turning inside the MiG more and more, this being one characteristic that our fighter definitely had over the faster enemy.

'Finally, when we had him in range, I opened up with three bursts but nothing seemed to happen. Suddenly, he started in a dive with me right on his tail. I gave him a couple more bursts on the way down. Fire was now coming from the MiG and we followed until he hit the ground in a massive explosion. In looking back on this, when we made a pass through the searchlights, the pilot of the MiG would turn off his wing lights and I could only assume that at that point he would accelerate, make a 180-degree turn, and head back toward our plane, at which time he would turn on his wing lights again. We went through the searchlight three times and on the fourth time, we got him."

Dunn had scored the Skyknight's fourth MiG kill, but it did not prevent enemy pilots from making aggressive attempts to shoot down B-29s at night. On 28 January, Capt James R Weaver's F3D-2 claimed another MiG, and three days later Lt Col Robert F Conley downed the sixth and final Skyknight kill of the war. He had just taken command of VMF(N)-513 from Lt Col Hutchinson, and his MiG also counted as the tenth, and final, aerial kill for all USMC nightfighters.

On 17 January 1953 another VMF(N)-513 Skyknight pilot, Capt George Kross, tangled with a MiG in a duel which tested his F3D's structural strength to the limit and made him a target in his opponents gun-

The sixth, and final, Skynight kill in Korea fell, rather appropriately, to VMF(N)-513's last wartime CO, Lt Col Robert F Conley. Again he was protecting B-29s from marauding MiG-15s when he claimed a single Russian fighter. The basic flying equipment worn by Marine fighter pilots of the period is perfectly illustrated in this posed shot of Conley, taken soon after his 31 January 1953 victory

sight. Kross recalls, 'My radar operator, MSgt J A Piekutowski, and I were flying cover for B-29s that were bombing targets up close to the Yalu River. My tail warning radar malfunctioned just about the time our ground control sent out a 'heads up' warning as they picked up several fast-moving MiGs that were in the vicinity of the bomber formation.

'Our F3D was above the stream at 30,000 ft. Suddenly, I felt cannon fire striking the aircraft. I went into a "split-S", with both throttles wide open, and within a few seconds I was able to get into an overcast at 20,000 ft under IFR (instrument flight rules) conditions, in a vertical dive. As I started to ease out of the dive, I found no elevator response! I could move the control stick forward and aft, yet nothing happened. My first thought was that the MiG's cannon fire had severed the control cables. I also noted that the airspeed indicator was far beyond the red limited speed marker. The aircraft hit about 750 mph, or Mach 1.02'. This speed was at least 150 mph faster than the portly Skyknight was intended to fly!

'My aircraft had gone beyond its limiting Mach number and the shock wave was blanking out the tail surfaces! I cut the throttle back to idle and put the speed brakes out. This caused an intense longitudinal wallowing as the speed brakes would open, collapse, and open full again. As my speed decreased, elevator control was regained. I went through several high speed stalls in trying to round out my recovery and succeeded in returning to level flight below the overcast and just above the Yellow Sea. Indicated airspeed was about 400 kts with idle throttle settings and dive brakes still fully extended. As we got into better weather conditions, I pulled up to 10,000 ft and went to slow flight and tried the landing gear and flaps, executing a stall just to be sure that I would have full control in the landing approach to Kunsan.'

Kross nursed the F3D home with several cannon holes in its tail and a hit between its two engines which had cut through 19 fuselage stringers before finally making impact with the escape hatch door located between the pilot and radar observer. If this wasn't bad enough, it's unlikely that either man would have been able to use the jet's downward ejection seats had it been necessary to get out, and this damage had come within inches of destroying an engine, which would have been fatal. The gruelling encounter told the Allied brass what the USMC fliers had known already – some nocturnal MiG-15s were equipped with air intercept radar.

In January 1953, the best-known Sabre pilot names were to include Fernandez, McConnell, Heller, Overton and Fischer. Lt Col Edwin L Heller, commander of the 16th FIS, bagged two MiG-15s on 22 January 1953. His Korean score was to end at 3.5 kills, adding to 5.5 victories claimed with the Eighth Air Force during World War 2.

On 24 January, Capts Dolphin D Overton III and Harold E Fischer, Jr, both of the 51st FIW, became the 24th and 25th US jet aces. Fischer belonged to the wing's 39th FIS and had flown a tour in F-80s before the Sabre. His F-86 was *PAPER TIGER*, a spanking-new F-86F-10-NA (51-12958) with the '6-3' hard wing retrofitted in place of the leading-edge slats it had been built with.

Overton was in the 16th FIS and was pilot of an F-86 named *DOLPH'S DEVIL* (on the jet's right side, crew chief A/2C Wilbur Cothron had added a second nickname, *ANGEL IN DISGUISE*). Overton, like Fischer, attained ace status after a tour in fighter-bombers – 102

The F-84-equipped 8th FBS 'Black Sheep' of the 49th FBW (commanded by Col John B Holt) pose for a group portrait which of includes 1949 West Point alumnus, 1st Lt Dolphin D Overton III (second row, far right), who flew 102 missions in the Thunderjet before going on to fly a further 48 in the F-86. On 24 January 1953, after shifting to a Sabre squadron (the 16th FIS/51st FIW, commanded by Lt Col Edwin Heller), Dolph Overton became the Korean War's 24th US air ace *(Col John B Holt)*

Although not the best quality shot to be taken in Korea, this view is nevertheless crucial to the story of the conflict's aces as it shows one of the two *HELL-ER BUST* F-86Es flown by the legendary Lt Col Edwin Heller, CO of the infamous 16th FIS/51st FIW. The jet wears the double blue nose stripes to denote that it is indeed the CO's aircraft, plus a small shark's mouth aft of the intake *(Dick Geiger)*

combat missions in the F-84, followed by 48 in the F-86. His first kill came on his 144th mission. During his final four sorties in the Sabre, billed at the time as 'the hottest streak in jet fighting history', Overton racked up five kills in the shortest period on record.

Overton's squadron commander was that aggressive fighter leader, Lt Col Heller, who flew at least two different F-86s nicknamed *HELL-ER BUST* – his P-51B of almost a decade before had been christened with the same nickname. Pilots in Heller's 16th FIS were regularly crossing the Yalu and jumping MiGs inside Manchuria. This was in violation of the rules, but it was also accepted practice – everybody was doing it. 'They were coming back with blackened gun ports after every sortie', recalls one officer. 'That meant they were shooting at MiGs every time they went up. That couldn't happen unless they were on the wrong side of the border'.

Another 51st FIW members recalls seeing gun camera films of a kill during this period. 'The MiG had his landing gear down and you could see that he was on final approach to land on the main runway at Antung. Those .50 cal bullets sawed off his right wing and sent it flipping around through the air, with the lowered landing wheel easily visible'. A third officer in the wing remembers, 'This was one of those periods when everybody was MiG crazy. They were willing to take chances, willing to bend the rules'. This comment was made in reference not to the entire 51st FIW, but specifically to its 16th FIS.

On one such mission which took pilots deep into Manchuria – the exact date is a matter of dispute – Overton shot down two more MiGs (his sixth and seventh), although he was never credited with their destruction. On the same sortie Heller was shot down, a burst of well-aimed cannon fire from a MiG-15 braking his right arm, severing his control stick and disabling his ejection seat. After an uncontrollable dive from 40,000 ft (12,384 m), Heller was at low altitude when he spotted an eight-inch shell hole in his canopy. He went through the gap and glanced off his Sabre's horizontal stabiliser on the way out. His 'chute opened just in time. One officer back at base recalls talk of a Rescue Combat Air Patrol mission; 'We took a look at a map and saw where he was. He was 150 miles north of the Yalu, so there was no rescue attempt'.

Overton's sixth and seventh kills and Heller's bailout – all north of the proscribed border – were witnessed by communist truce negotiators aboard a train nearby. In wonderment, Eastern European diplomats watched Heller's parachute descend to earth. He was to be subjected to horrible mistreatment by his Chinese captors, who tried to get him to 'confess' not only to crossing the border but to doing so on the express orders of his commanders.

Among these was 51st FIW boss (and ace), Col John W Mitchell, who learned of border crossings and, as one officer remembers, 'was madder than any colonel I've ever seen'. Mitchell learned that four-ship flights had been heading north

consisting of four men who were all qualified flight leaders. An airman remembers, 'we had a big flap. The day after Heller was shot down, an L-5 arrives at Suwon and there's Gen Barcus, commander of the Fifth Air Force, arriving to confab with Mitchell and raising hell'. Mitchell and Barcus made some immediate personnel changes, but as military services often do, they also chose a scapegoat – the relatively junior Capt Dolph D Overton III, who had graduated from West Point in 1949, flown 150 F-84 and F-86 missions, downed seven MiGs – and followed routine, everyday orders just like everybody else when he flew into China with Heller. Col Mitchell chose a surrogate, group commander Col Brooks, to inform Overton that he was to be stripped of ace status and shipped out of Korea immediately.

The attempt to transform Overton into a 'non-ace' was rejected by higher headquarters, but his final kills were never approved and Overton eventually left the Air Force. A man of quick wit and great charm, he is incapable of being bitter, but when he and Heller met to discuss these events for the first time 41 years later, they had much to learn about from others who'd been there – neither was at Suwon when Col Mitchell 'stood down' the 16th FIS for several days and read the riot act to its pilots.

Before the shakeup, another 'deuce act' was achieved by Capt Cecil G Foster, also of Heller's 16th FIS, who shot down two MiG-15s on 24 January 1953. Ironically, the success of January's air battles with MiGs, including those north of the forbidden border, almost certainly helped break the logjam in the armistice talks.

It was kind of an afterthought when, on 30 January, Lt Raymond J Kinsey of the 4th FIW shot down the first Tu-2 bomber to be spotted in more than a year. That day, 1st Lt Joseph M McConnell, Jr, got a MiG – he bagged another the next day. On 31 January F-94B pilot Capt Ben Fithian and radar operator 1st Lt Sam Lyons made the first official kill credited to the 319th FIS. Their vanquished opponent is thought to have been a La-9, but is listed in the official record merely as a 'prop'.

Fithian recalls, 'It was a clear, cold, night at K-13 (Suwon air base). My RO, Sam Lyons, and I were on alert, standing about third in the "scramble" order. We heard through intelligence that there was heavy enemy air activity over North Korea. About that time, a call came in from K-13 tower asking us to scramble one of our aircraft to pace an F-80 in for a

This handclasp is dated 24 January 1953, and shows Capt Overton III (right) of the 16th FIS/51st FIW shaking hands with crew chief A/2C Wilbur Cothron after the former had shot down his fifth MiG-15. Overton's F-86 had the name *DOLPH'S DEVIL* on the left (pilot's) side and *ANGEL IN DISGUISE* on the right (crew chief's) side. Armourer on this Sabre was A/2C Robert S Baldwin. Overton wears an exposure suit, which was typical 'fighter-jock' attire during the frigid Korean winter. *DOLPH'S DEVIL/ANGEL IN DISGUISE* was an early F-86E-1-NA, serialled 50-631 *(USAF via Wilbur Cothron)*

landing. The jet, an 8th FBW bird, had lost its air speed indicator. We were selected to do the job. After getting airborne, it took about 15 minutes to locate, join up, and help the F-80 back to the base. We were too heavy on fuel to land so we changed to a tactical channel and requested to be vectored into North Korea. Since one of our jets on station near Cho-do Island was having trouble with its radar, they accepted our request'. By this time, the FEAF had eased up on its restrictions on operating the F-94B, with its classified APC-33 air intercept radar, over enemy territory.

'On the way in', Fithian continues, 'I heard the F-94B ahead of us calling "no joy", which meant they could not establish radar contact. In fact, the pilot was complaining that he thought Cho-do was vectoring them in on rocks projecting from the sea. When we got within about 50 miles of the activity, Cho-do released the other F-94B for recovery to K-13 taking control of us. We were at about 25,000 ft when the controller started giving us range and direction to a "bogey". It was something like 30 miles at one o'clock. They gave us a descent order to 5000 ft and a series of turns. We ended up at 5000 ft going southeast about 10 to 15 miles west of Pyongyang, the capital of North Korea. We were six miles behind the hostile, who was doing about 130 kts. We swung in behind the bogey and continued to descend, making our first radar contact at about five miles.

'In order to get the optimum advantage with our airborne radar fire control system, we descended to tree top level. It was a moonlit night and I could see the ground under us, but not ahead. Once, I looked out and we were very close to some trees that looked like tall poplars or sycamores, so I climbed up just a bit. I figured that the pilot probably knew the terrain well and if he could get through, we could, too. Also, the prize of the "first kill" using the F-94B was worth laying it all on the line. We made radar contact at about five miles and slowed down to 130 kts. With speed brakes extended – after getting a lock on the bogey – we started to close and climb slightly since the target was actually at about 1200 ft altitude.

'I started firing on the radar scope. I fired a long burst and saw no results. We continued to close and I fired again. Still no hits. We were about 600 ft behind the target and I moved the stick around in about a six-inch circle and saw some flashes. We were armed with API, and they made a flash upon impact. As soon as I saw a lot of flashes, I held the stick steady and continued to fire. The enemy aircraft burst into flames and started down. He crashed with the cockpit closed.

'We called "splash one" and Cho-do gave us a vector towards another bogie about eight miles away. We were low on fuel due to our escorting the F-80 at the beginning of the flight. Our altitude was still very low and we ran into some automatic weapons fire. As we climbed out of it, my RO said we had a fire in the rear cockpit. I thought at first we had been hit by ground fire, but it turned out to be an electrical short which went away when the rear cockpit light was turned off.

'On recovery at K-13, we did a victory roll and landed. We were met in the revetment by almost everyone in the 319th. When we shut our engine off, everybody clapped their hands. After that night, it was several months before the North Koreans flew at night or at least were detected by our radar at Cho-do Island. The next time they got active, a brave young crew from my flight, Lts Wilcox and Goldberg, apparently shot one down over the water and then either crashed into the sea or hit the enemy aircraft.

Far Right Like Col Thyng, his predecessor as commander of the 4th FIW, Col James K Johnson is one of the great US fighter leaders who never received nearly enough recognition. This portrait of double aces represents 54 MiG-15s destroyed in combat over the Yalu River. They are, left to right; Capt Lonnie Moore (10 MiGs); Lt Col Vermont Garrison (10); wing commander Johnson (10); Capt Ralph Parr (nine MiGs and one Il-2); and Maj James Jabara (15 MiGs). In the background is Johnson's F-86F Sabre (51-12941), which, despite wearing nine of its pilot's ten kills, was only used to shoot down a small percentage of this total (USAF)

Capts Joseph McConnell and Harold Fischer stand in front of the former's first BEAUTIOUS BUTCH (F-86E 51-2753) at Suwon airfield in early 1953. Both belonged to the 39th FIS/51st FIW. McConnell was later shot down and rescued in the Yellow Sea, before going on to become the ranking American ace of the Korean War with 16 victories. Hal Fischer flew an F-86F-10-NA named PAPER TIGER (51-12958), and had scored 10 aerial kills prior to being shot down and captured north of the Yalu River (via Bill Hess)

They called "splash", and that was the last we ever heard from them."

On 16 February 1st Lt Joseph M McConnell, Jr, of the 39th FIS/51st FIW shot down his fifth MiG. Because of a delay in confirmation, he became the 27th ace of the war. Capt Manuel J 'Pete' Fernandez, Jr of the 334th FIS/4th FIW was recognised as the 26th ace when he claimed his fifth and sixth kills on 18 February. Lt Col Royal N Baker's score of 13 kills made him the leading surviving ace of the conflict at the time.

On 27 March, Maj James P Hagerstrom flamed two MiG-15s. His eventual score was to be 8.5. Though his first two kills were scored with the 334th FIS/4th FIW, Hagerstrom claimed the remainder while flying new F-86F Sabres with the 67th FBS/18th FBG, which had converted to the new jet that very month; he was to become the 18th FBW's only ace. On 28 March Col James K Johnson, 4th FIW boss, bagged two MiGs to become the 29th US ace in Korea – he also had a kill from World War 2. The next day Lt Col George L Jones (4th FIG commander) became the 30th. Also in March Fernandez accounted for four more MiG-15s, capping his fighting frenzy with two kills in one day.

METEOR FINALE

On the same day that Maj Hagerstrom opened his account, No 77 Sqn closed theirs with the Meteor's fourth, and last, confirmed MiG kill of the war. The jet fell to the guns of Sgt George Hale, who was flying 'his' F.8, A77-851, which bore the nickname *"HALESTORM"* (the forward fuselage of this jet is still in existence in a museum in Australia). He had been part of a four-aircraft section (led by the unit's OC, Sqn Ldr J Hubble) sent to attack installations along the Pyongyang-Singosan road.

On reaching the junction at Namch'onjom, the formation split, with Hale and his wingman, Sgt Irlam, heading south. Flying in line astern formation at low-level, they soon spotted two RF-80s being chased by a pair of MiG-15s. Hale immediately 'punched' off his ventral tank and turned hard into the enemy. His aircraft still had two High Velocity Aerial Rockets (HVARs) attached to their pylons so he fired them at the MiGs – they passed between the two jets, which immediately broke left and right.

Hale tracked the jet that had headed north, and as Irlam tried to stay with him, he felt hits to his F.8. Responding to his wingman's urgent call for help, Hale forgot

Below A busy seen at Kimpo in the spring of 1953 as most of No 77 Sqn's Meteor F.8s are fuelled up prior to their next ground attack strikes. Parked at the head of the ramp behind the bowsers is A77-851, better known as Sgt George Hale's *"HALESTORM"*. This jet was used by him to claim the squadron's fourth, and last, MiG kill of the war on 27 March 1953. Amazingly, the forward fuselage section of this fighter resides today intact in the Warbirds Aviation Museum in Mildura, New South Wales. Having survived in Korea for over a year, -851 served with No 23 Sqn at Amberley, in Queensland, before being one of 15 F.8s converted to U.21A drone configuration. It crash landed at Woomera in late 1963 while operating in this capacity, and only the cockpit section survived the scrapper's torch once it had been struck of charge *(No 77 Sqn via Tony Fairbairn)*

Serving with No 77 Sqn concurrently with Sgt George Hale was Flt Lt 'Willie' Williamson, one of several RAF exchange officers assigned to the unit in the last months of the war. Later to become Air Marshal Sir Keith Williamson, he is seen here climbing into his personal F.8, *No Sweat!*, at Kimpo in October 1953 *(Roy Royston via Tony Fairbairn)*

about the fleeing MiG and pulled around to discover that two other jets had attacked them out of the sun. Whilst Irlam headed for nearby cloud cover, Hale turned into his assailant, who in the meantime had extended his airbrakes in order to reduce speed and slot in behind the former's crippled Meteor. However, the MiG pilot still overshot, and Hale in turn repeated his quarry's manoeuvre, but to greater effect. He was now in an ideal position astern of the slowed MiG, and he let rip with the F.8's four 20 mm cannon. The MiG was hit behind the cockpit and it rolled onto its back and lost height, spewing black smoke.

Hale was about to follow it down when two more MiGs attacked him from above. He pulled hard into them and fired, but their high-speed dive carried them safely away. However, a further pair then appeared on Hale's tail and he again turned into them, scoring hits on the trailing jet, which left a trail of white smoke (or possibly fuel) in its wake. He was now out of ammunition and the MiG escaped to fight another day. Upon his return to Kimpo, Hale discovered that his wingman's jet had no less than 112 shrapnel holes in it. His own jet wore two MiG silhouettes beneath its cockpit for a short time, courtesy of his crew chief, Bob Cherry – these were soon painted out, however, on the strict instructions of Sqn Ldr Hubble as they contravened RAAF regulations.

The MiGs were busy in April, 1st Lt Joe McConnell claiming his eighth kill, but he was also shot down. Plucked from the Yellow Sea by a 3rd Air Rescue Group Sikorsky H-19 helicopter, McConnell was promoted to captain two weeks later. He soon became a double ace.

In the spring of 1953, Johnson's 4th FIW played host to Project *Gun Val*, which brought eight F-86F Sabres, equipped with four 20 mm cannon rather than the usual six .50 calibre machine-guns, to Korea for combat evaluation. Details of this programme have never emerged, but *Gun Val* was apparently part of a larger Air Force programme to evaluate 20 mm cannon, the weapon favoured by the Navy, against the .50 calibre machine guns which were standard within the USAF. Two or three MiG-

Capt Manuel J 'Pete' Fernandez, Jr, wearing the winged pigeon (which later became an eagle) emblem of the 334th FIS, holds a sign reporting on his aerial victory credits as of the day this portrait was snapped. 'MiGs HAVA YES' is a GI version of the Korean language's grammatical structure and means, simply, 'We have MiGs'. Fernandez's final score was 14.5 victories *(USAF)*

Left The last unit to transition from F-80s to F-86s in Korea was the seasoned 8th FBW at Suwon. Being last did have its advantages in this case, however, as the wing was issued with brand new F-86F models. Despite being the ultimate dogfighting version of the Sabre to see service in the conflict, the 8th FBW had little chance to prove its mettle over the Yalu as the wing was tasked almost exclusively with close-air support missions in conjunction with UN troops on the ground. This impressive line up of 35th FBS jets is headed by the multi-coloured F-86-30-NA of wing boss, Col W B Wilmet. Behind his machine is the unit commanders F-86F *(James Carter via Jerry Scutts)*

15s are thought to have been shot down by *Gun Val*'s Sabres.

As most squadrons were now equipped with the F-86F, Col James K Johnson was able to say to a group of his pilots in March 1953 that they now had a fighter which was 'practically equal' to the MiG-15, with the caveat that the Sabre had to be maintained in top condition by all-important ground personnel.

In April, a MiG pilot shot down the 51st Wing's Capt Harold E Fischer who was, by now, a ten-kill double ace. Fischer was across the Yalu in Manchuria when he was downed and taken prisoner. He, like Heller, became a PoW not in North Korea but in China, and they were not released until two years after the war. By the end of the month, Capt Fernandez had downed his 11th MiG to remain one kill ahead of Capt McConnell, but still two behind the total of 13 attained by Col Baker.

On 3 May, an unknown prop-driven fighter was credited to F-94B pilot 2nd Lt Stanton G Wilcox of the 319th FIS. This was the mission referred to in an earlier quote by fellow F-94B pilot Fithian. Wilcox, and his back-seater, did not return from the mission, being lost to unknown causes. On 10 May, the night-fighting F-94Bs of the 319th FIS finally toted up their first MiG kill – Capt John R Phillips was the pilot and 1st Lt Billy J Atto the radar observer.

Capt Phillips describes the mission. 'Squadron operations figured that if we could start sending a flight up north around three or four o'clock in the morning, we just might catch the enemy south of the Yalu. On the 10th, we were flying just such a mission. The weather was poor with visibility about 300 ft in heavy rain. We launched with no problems. Heading north, we checked in with Cho-do. They told us there were heavy "tracks" south of the big Chinese base at Antung, so we climbed up to 40,000 ft until we got in the area, then eased down to around 30,000 ft – it had taken us nearly 20 minutes to climb to the higher altitude. At about this time, Atto picked up two bogeys on his scope. We started to move down on them, calling JOC (Joint Operations Center) through Cho-do, but we couldn't get permission to fire. We kept calling and trying to keep lined up on the two targets. Finally, we got the go-ahead to fire. The exhaust patterns were very distinct and they were MiGs.

'We started firing and the two bogeys split up with us going after the one on the left. The second one came around behind us to set up for a firing pass. We held our position and before we shot down our target, the other MiG had a lock on us. After several bursts of .50-cal rounds into the first MiG, there was a terrific flash of fire as he exploded. The concentration of the second MiG pilot was sidetracked: he immediately broke off and headed for home. Atto looked up from his scope and saw flaming debris passing by off the right wing of our F-94. When the encounter was over, we were below 15,000 ft and encountering ground fire, so we set a course for K-13. When we arrived in the area, the ceiling was now at 500 ft, so we were able to land without diverting to Japan as we had originally thought we would. The "kill" was made over Pukchin, North Korea.'

Only the front-seater in the F-94B was credited with an aerial victory and Phillips' is officially listed not as a MiG-15, but simply as a 'jet'.

Also on 10 May, while escorting fighter-bombers, Capt Fernandez shot down a MiG and shared credit for another. Added to a pair of additional kills in May, he now had 14.5 victories, and was now the top-scoring US ace of the conflict. Fernandez was not an imposing figure and was mild-mannered – scarcely the Hollywood 'jet jock' needed on recruiting posters. It's impossible to confirm, but is rumoured that among the top brass, *somebody* didn't want the leading ace to have a 'foreign-sounding' name. In the culture of the period, McConnell was not 'foreign-sounding', a fact which may have been of immeasurable help to Fernandez's chief competitor when he begged not to be sent home.

It was Joe McConnell's own ability, however, which brought about the unprecedented feat of bagging three MiGs in one day. After claiming a trio of MiGs in early May, Capt McConnell went on to shoot down a further two between dawn and dusk on 18 May 1953. This raised his tally to 16 kills, putting him, finally and forever, ahead of Pete Fernandez.

Fernandez's great rival, Capt Joseph M McConnell, Jr, of the 39th FIS/51st FIW, cinches his seatbelt in a L-20A Beaver which will carry him from Suwon to Kimpo to catch a transport home to America. McConnell is wearing the standard overseas cap, starched khakis and non-regulation brogan boots. 'I want that man out of Suwon and on his way back home', barked Lt Gen Barcus, the FEAF boss, who worried that an ace with 16 kills ought not to be exposed to further prospect of injury or death. With three MiGs downed in a single day on 18 May 1953, McConnell's tally of 16 made him the UN's 'ace of aces'. He was later killed in a postwar crash while testing an F-86H at Edwards AFB, California *(USAF via R L Gonterman)*

McConnell's was to remain the record for the war, and was to make him its 'ace of aces'. But his pleas for more fell on deaf ears – 18 May was also the day Lt Col George I Ruddell, commander of the 39th FIS, and pilot of an F-86F called *MiG MAD MAVIS* (51-12940), destroyed his fifth MiG to become the 31st ace of the war. That same day, Lt Col Louis A Green (336th FIS) bagged two MiGs, to repeat McConnell's feat.

It was, however, the latter's last day in air combat. Gen Barcus, fearful of the consequences if he should lose his top MiG-killer, is reported to have proclaimed, 'I want that man on his way back home to the United States of America before you hear the period at the end of this sentence'. McConnell reportedly packed his B-4 bag in minutes while an L-20 Beaver waited, propeller turning over, to take him up to Kimpo to catch a transport home. Fernandez ended up in third place among US aces after James Jabara (of whom, more shortly) finished with 15 victories.

On 26 May, Jabara, who had returned for a second tour of duty in the combat zone (again with the 334th FIS), was leading a flight of four Sabres when he sighted 16 MiGs crossing the Yalu near Uiju. Jabara led his flight into the centre of the jets, scattered them, and then pounced on a pair of MiGs which hadn't gotten out of the way fast enough. Jabara quickly forced one MiG into a fatal spin and shot down another, the eighth and ninth aerial victories for the war's original American ace.

Overall, in less than two years the Sabre pilot had gone from underdog to victor. Once outnumbered and outflown, he was no longer seriously challenged. The supremacy of the F-86 in the skies was in stark contrast to the deteriorating situation on the ground, where the Chinese were gradually poking a hole in UN lines and threatening a major break-through.

On 7 June, the the 319th FIS (F-94Bs) racked up their third and final aerial victory, a MiG-15 – pilot was Lt Col Robert V McHale. Lt Col Vermont Garrison, who commanded the 335th FIS, scored two kills on 5 June 1953 to become the 32nd American ace – at the decrepit age, for a fighter pilot, of 37. Garrison had been credited with 7.33 victories in World War 2 flying with a sister squadron, the 336th. Capts Lonnie R Moore and Ralph S Parr became the 33rd and 34th aces on 18 June.

Col Robert P Baldwin, 51st FIG commander, became the 35th ace on 22 June 1953, and eight days later 1st Lt Henry 'Hank' Buttelmann became the 36th American ace, and the youngest (although not the most junior) at the age of 23. His eventual tally was seven.

Also, by the end of June 1953 Maj Jabara had run his kill tally up to 14, putting him within two MiGs of Capt McConnell's top-ranking score, and within half a kill of Capt Fernandez as the war's second-ranking ace. In a month of fighting which shattered all previous records, Sabres shot down 77 MiG-15s, including a record 16 in a single day on 30 June.

In July 1953, two 4th FIW F-86 pilots, Capt Clyde A Curtin and Maj Stephen L Bettinger, became the 38th and 39th American air aces. The latter was shot down and taken prisoner soon after scoring his fifth kill, and although his wingman reported his aerial victory, two further witnesses were required, so Bettinger was not confirmed as an ace until released from captivity on 2 October 1953.

In July 1953, 4th FIW F-86 pilot Capt Clyde A Curtin became the 38th American fighter ace of the Korean War. This subsequent November 1957 portrait shows the now Maj Curtin at a pre-flight briefing whilst serving as CO of the 450th Fighter Day Squadron *(USAF)*

Looking remarkably fresh due to a lack of kill markings and gaudy nose art, 52-2882 was one of 60 Canadair F-86E-6-CANs – equivalent to the RCAF's Sabre Mk 2 – built for use by US forces (including their Canadian exchange pilots) in Korea. Like all F-86As, -Es and some -Fs, this jet has wing leading-edge slats which improved low-speed performance, but offered no advantages in air combat. It wears the 'checkerboard' tail adopted by the 51st FIW, plus the red trim of the 25th FIS. It was one of several F-86s flown by 1st Lt Hank Buttelmann, who became the 36th, and youngest, US ace (although not the most junior) on 30 June 1953 at the age of 23. His final score was seven *(Henry Buttelmann)*

Of the 40 Americans who attained ace status in Korea, only one did not fly Sabres – the Navy's Lt Guy P 'Lucky Pierre' Bordelon, pilot of a F4U-5NL (BuNo 124453, coded 'NP-21' of VC-3) which operated from ashore and racked up five prop-driven 'Bedcheck Charlie' kills – the Fifth Air Force had requested piston-engined assistance from the Navy to help curb the enemy's nocturnal activities, as its own F-94Bs couldn't operate at such low speeds. Bordelon's kill list covers a pair of Yak-18s on both 29 June and 1 July 1953, and a Lavochkin fighter of unspecified type on 17 July – a very rapid streak of aerial victories. Sadly, the only 'ace' Corsair was wrecked in a mishap by another pilot just as the war ended.

Before the truce was signed on 27 July 1953, Maj Jabara toted up his 15th kill to pass Fernandez and become the war's second-ranking MiG killer and, with McConnell, one of just two triple aces. On 22 July F-86 pilot 1st Lt Sam P Young of the 51st FIW racked up the final MiG kill of the war. The armistice was signed on 27 July to take place 12 hours after signature. Meanwhile, at mid-morning one patrol sighted 12 dark green MiGs near the Yalu, but the communist pilots high-tailed it for the river before the F-86s could engage. Shortly after noon, Capt Ralph S Parr shot down an Ilyushin Il-12 transport, after making two passes to be certain he was not making an identification mistake. Its destruction caused a diplomatic protest, and made Parr a double ace. It was also the last kill of the war.

During the Korean War, the USAF lost 971 aircraft and the Navy and Marine Corps 1033, but fewer than ten per cent of these fell in air-to-air combat. Communist figures for losses are not available, but according to US numbers the other side lost 792 MiGs in air-to-air combat, with another 143 were listed as probably destroyed. Many years after the war, a study by the Air Force, code-named *Sabre Measures Charlie*, downgraded the F-86-versus-MiG-15 'kill ratio' from 14-1 to 7-1 – the latter figure is not disputed by Russian participants. Although reduced, the 'kill ratio' achieved by Sabre pilots is still truly remarkable when one considers how totally outnumbered they were throughout the entire conflict.

Lt Guy P 'Lucky Pierre' Bordelon of VC-3 became the US Navy's only Korean War ace after a brief spell of action in mid-1953 – he was duly awarded the Navy Cross (second only to the Medal of Honor) as the pilot of this F4U-5NL Corsair (BuNo 124453, coded 'NP-21') for his exploits. Other VC-3 nightfighters sailed with every American carrier deployed to Korea, but the only other air-to-air kills were three Yaks credited to Navy F4U-4s, and a MiG-15 downed by a Marine Corps F4U-4B – both versions of Corsair were operating as day fighters. Though difficult to see in this right-side view, Bordelon's aircraft has five red stars painted in a row beneath its cockpit (*Jeff Ethell via Jim Sullivan*)

Lt Guy Bordelon's unique F4U-5NL was comprehensively wrecked by another pilot around the time of the armistice. His machine was later scrapped in situ (*via Jim Sullivan*)

SOVIET ACES AND THE MiG-15

This MiG-15bis was flown down to Kimpo at low-level by defecting North Korean Peoples Air Force pilot Ro Kim Suk on 21 September 1953, just weeks after the war had finished – the pilot received $100,000 from the US government as payment for his 'gift'. Given the USAF serial 2015337, it quickly had its national markings painted over with a more familiar 'star and bar', after which it was dismantled and freighted to Kadena, on the island of Okinawa, and thoroughly evaluated by a team of Air Force test pilots that included Maj Chuck Yeager and Capt Tom Collins. The official caption that was released with this USAF photograph in October 1953 ends with a statement that perfectly sums up the West's attitude towards Soviet equipment throughout the four decades of Cold War. 'After a week of testing which included simulated combat with F-86 "Sabre" jets, they (the test team) said the MiG-15 did not measure up to the F-86.' One can only guess as to what the likes of Collins and Yeager really thought *(USAF via Jerry Scutts)*

The twin revolutions of *Perestroika* (restructuring) and *Glasnost* (openness) which swept through Soviet society during the late 1980s quickly led to chinks being revealed in the old 'Iron Curtain'. This new-found openness did not, however, extend that far back into history, and although a handful of Soviet participants in Korea broke their silence, details of the overall Soviet participation in the conflict remain sketchy to this day. The 40 years that have elapsed since the end of the war have allowed the traditional accounts to become entrenched, such that the version of events written by the USAF at the height of the Cold War is widely regarded as the only truth. Those who have sought to question that history are disparagingly labelled as revisionists, regarded with some suspicion and have had their motives questioned.

New information from Russia reveals that the long-accepted victory claims by UN pilots are exaggerated, and that estimates of losses to enemy fighter action are even more wildly under-estimated. This does not, however, diminish the achievements of the UN fighter pilots in Korea, since it replaces their traditional image as easy victors against a second rate enemy, with a greater achievement as victors over a formidable and well-equipped enemy. Nor does it reflect any widespread dishonesty on the part of those Allied pilots who did claim kills. Generally fighting over enemy held territory, the UN pilots could not rely on obtaining aircraft wreckage to back-up pilots' evidence or gun camera film, and the verification of victory claims was inevitably based on loose criteria.

Also, many jets that appeared to be mortally wounded actually limped home to fight again another day due to the light calibre of the Sabre's

guns. The first MiG shot down in Korea reportedly absorbed nearly 1000 rounds before it succumbed, for example. 'The US Browning .50 cal guns acted on our aircraft like peas', said leading Soviet ace Yevgeni Pepelyaev, dismissively. 'It was routine for our aircraft to return home having taken 40 or 50 hits'. The MiG-15 was certainly extremely well protected against small-calibre fire, with effective self-sealing fuel tanks, an armoured windscreen and excellent cockpit armour behind the pilot.

In the aftermath of the war, the USAF admitted only 58 F-86 losses in aerial combat, and 971 losses overall (mostly to AAA and non-operational causes), while the Russians themselves (not including the Korean and Chinese MiG units) claimed 1300 kills. The USAF claimed 792 MiGs shot down, while Russian sources admit only 345 losses (to all causes, and conceivably not including Korean and Chinese flown aircraft). Postwar revisions reduced USAF claims to 379 MiG-15s and increased admitted F-86 losses to 103. The latter figure is probably rather low, although it could bring a total MiG-15:F-86 kill ratio close to 3.5:1, with a 1:1 ratio being conceivable if F-80s and F-84s were brought into the equation.

In fairness, it needs to be pointed out that one should also avoid taking Russian claims at face value, without question. Although the corroboration of victory claims may have been tighter on the Russian side than on the American, it is equally certain that some Russian victory claims were made and accepted for engagements in which no UN aircraft was actually lost, and that the widespread misidentification of UN aircraft types resulted in almost every F-84 kill (and many an F-80 kill) being written up as an 'F-86'. If Soviet figures are accepted as being as reliable as those of the USAF, however, it becomes clear that the communist side included the two top-scoring aces of the conflict – Yevgeni Pepelyaev with 23 kills, and Nikolai Sutyagin with 21 – and at least 16 pilots with ten or more.

Whatever the exact kill and loss figures, it is clear that the UN and communist air forces were much more closely matched than has been thought previously, and that while the F-86 pilots did enjoy an advantage, it was a narrow one, making survival itself (to say nothing of an air-to-air victory) a worthy achievement. Whilst it is debatable whether or not the Russian pilots enjoyed much success against the Sabres of the 4th and 51st FIWs, the MiG certainly enjoyed devastating success against fighter-bombers like the F-80, F-84 and Meteor, which were generally inferior to the MiG, and which often operated in large formations.

Senior Russian officers have averred that protecting North Korea from raids by fighter-bombers was the primary role of MiG-15s in Korea, and that they engaged F-86s 'only when they prevented us from breaking through to the bombers, or when we encountered them accidentally. Chinese and North Korean MiG-15s had a much more difficult time with the Sabres', said one. Sometimes fighter-bombers would simply try to avoid combat, but at other times would successfully stay and fight. 'Often a rendezvous (with enemy fighter-bombers) became a short, stubborn, engagement in which we and they lost men and aircraft', recalled Georgy Lobov, former commander of the Soviet air forces in Korea.

Some of the Soviet pilots deployed to Korea were of extremely high calibre. Many were aces in the Great Patriotic War, who were quickly able to regain old skills given the right training, while some of the younger men were even more effective. Moreover, they were highly motivated. Many genuinely believed that the UN forces were undertaking a war of aggression against North Korea, and the selective propaganda lent weight to the idea that the Americans were fighting with untold barbarism. Major-General Georgy Lobov (commander of the 64th Fighter Aviation Corps from 1952) was shown the aftermath of a B-29 raid on the town of Sinuiju even before he arrived in Korea to take up his first combat appointment – command of the 303rd IAD.

He recalls being 'involuntarily reminded' of Dresden, believing Sinuiju to have been a town of no military significance, representing US determination to wage war on the North Korean populace. Similarly, US plans to attack dams supplying Hydro-Electric Power stations were misreported as being plans to destroy water storage dams, which were aimed at hitting the native civilian population. Soviet pilots saw themselves as the protectors of North Korea against Imperialist aggression.

THE 'RIGHT' CAUSE

This belief that theirs' was the 'right' side was backed up by the understandable fear of the consequences of failure. Units (let alone individual pilots) could easily be sent home in disgrace if they made a poor showing, and anything which could be construed as being more serious than inefficiency or ineffectiveness could have threatened the safety of families left at home. Regimental political officers routinely warned Russian pilots that they would lose 'everything' if they were taken prisoner. Moreover, the MiG-15 itself inspired a degree of confidence, since it was in many respects more than equal to the USAF's best fighter, the F-86. Sergei Kramarenko, a squadron commander during in War, and an ace with 13 victories (to add to 12 scored during the Great Patriotic War), describes the two aircraft in the following passage.

'The Sabre was the most dangerous threat to my friends and I in Korean skies. Our MiG-15 and the F-86 belonged to the same class, similar types with similar performance. They differed only in that the MiG had an advantage in rate of climb at altitude, while the Sabre was superior in manoeuvring, especially at low level. These advantages could not always be used, however. The fight, as a rule, was decided in the first attack. After the first pass MiG-15s reached for altitude, while Sabres rushed for the ground. Each tried to reach the altitude where it held a distinct advantage, and thus the battle faded.'

In fact, the MiG-15 enjoyed some other advantages. While the F-86 had six fast-firing .50 calibre machine-guns, the MiG had three slow-firing heavy cannon; two NR-23 23 mm cannon and a single 37 mm N-37. These had a tremendous range, and each round had enormous destructive potential. The slow rate of fire of the N-37 made the heavier gun an ideal weapon for use against bomber targets, but against fast moving, manoeuvring fighters, accurate aiming was difficult. Nonetheless, one hit would often destroy an F-86, and many Soviet aces felt that the weapon was their biggest advantage. Unfortunately, the MiG-15 pilot was let down by his gunsight – the primitive ASP sight – which often failed during high-g manoeuvring, and which was not linked to any automatic ranging device (unlike that fitted to the Sabre, which used radar ranging).

The participation of the Soviet air forces (plural, because both Frontal Aviation and PVO air defence units were sent to Korea) differed in many ways to the USAF. Shrouded in secrecy in an effort to avoid widening the conflict, the USSR tried to hide its participation at all, attempting to forbid the use of Russian over the radio, and dressing many of its personnel in Chinese uniforms, without ranks or papers. Casualties were secretly buried in the old cemetery at Port Arthur, alongside those who had died in the 1904 Russo-Japanese war. Even to those who knew that Soviet pilots were fighting in Korea, the Soviet government maintained the pretence that its pilots in Korea were merely volunteers.

Just as UN fighter pilots were theoretically forbidden from hot-pursuits across the Yalu River, Soviet MiG-15 pilots were forbidden from flying over the sea, or from straying south of an imaginary line drawn between Wonsan and Pyongyang.

The Soviet participation in Korea was never large, the commander of the 64th IAD claiming that Soviet fighter strength in Korea never

reached that of the USAF's 4th and 51st Fighter Wings, although large numbers of MiG-15s were used, however ineffectually, by the Korean and Chinese air forces. At its peak, the Soviet 64th Fighter Aviation Corps in Korea parented three Fighter Aviation Divisions, all of which were under-strength, some with only two (instead of three) constituent regiments (which were similarly understrength), together with night fighter and naval aviation regiments. Because the 34 airfields south of the Yalu were attacked without respite by Allied fighter-bombers if ever it even looked as if they might be used, Soviet jets were restricted to using three strips north of the Yalu; Antung, Manpo and, from 1952, Tapao.

Units were rotated in and out of combat en masse (division by division), with only a brief period for the 'old hands' to pass on their experience to the new boys, and with no opportunity for experienced and inexperienced pilots to fly together, as was common practise in UN units. The very fact that Soviet fighters were operating in Korea was confidential, and this made it impossible to use lessons learned in combat to prepare other units before they arrived in-theatre. Units arrived having undergone dramatically different preparations, with the result that certain groups were much more successful than others.

For the Soviets, the war could be divided into three distinct phases. During the initial phase, UN air power had proved unstoppable. The North Korean air force was poorly trained and was equipped only with obsolescent piston-engined fighters like the Yak-9 and La-11. The so-

Although the USAF High Command could falsely deride the capabilities of the MiG-15, as well as the pilots that flew it, few could deny the damage that just a single well aimed 23 or 37 mm shell fired from the jet's battery of cannon could cause to the soft skin of a fast jet. No doubt subconciously thanking North American Aviation for building his F-86F particularly well, Lt William S O'Leary of the 35th FBS/8th FBW takes in the damage from ramp level back at base. The pilot had just dropped his bombs during a raid deep into North Korea when the MiG struck, but fortunately he managed to evade his assailant and fly back south. This photograph was taken in June 1953 *(USAF via Jerry Scutts)*

called 'Parade' regiment (the 29th IAP) from Kubinka had been deployed to China even before the war began, and was joined by the 151st IAD, coming under the control of the newly formed 64th Fighter Aviation Corps. They were committed to action from November 1950, and, flying from their bases north of the Yalu, were able to blunt the UN offensive.

Although the MiGs proved successful against ground attack aircraft, combat with the F-86 was one-sided. Pilots were ill-trained and used poor tactics, and the Hero of the Soviet Union order was awarded for the destruction of as few as three aircraft, with an Order of Lenin for the completion of 40 sorties. The second group rotated in to replace the original pilots had been better selected and prepared, and enjoyed greater success.

These were the 324th IAD, commanded by the great World War 2 ace, Ivan Kozhedub, and the 303rd IAD, under Georgy Lobov, who later became commander of the 64th IAK. The 324th IAD comprised the 176th GvIAP and the 196th IAP, two regiments containing a high proportion of experienced pilots from the Great Patriotic War, and arrived in Korea during March 1951. The 196th IAP, commanded by Yevgeni Pepelyaev, had trained hard before the deployment, its CO being a fierce believer in the adage 'train hard, fight easy'. Thus, Pepelyaev instituted intensive low level training, and drove his pilots to practise dogfighting in pairs, flights and larger formations. His stated aim was to 'strive to meet the American standard', and the result was that his pilots were what he called 'adequately prepared'. He felt that his was the only unit in Korea to be in such a position, and long after the war acknowledged that even his pilots, man for man, were not as well trained as the Americans they faced.

Nevertheless, during its tour, the 196th claimed 104 aircraft destroyed for the loss of 10 MiGs and four pilots – 23 of this total fell to the guns of Pepelyaev himself. The 176th GvIAP had an unhappy start, however, losing three jets during its first mission, but went on to claim 103 aircraft for the loss of 17 MiGs and five pilots. Both units operated from Antung.

THE 303RD IAD

Lobov's 303rd IAD was based at Manpo, and proved only marginally less successful than Kozhedub's Division, claiming a similar number of kills and losing 30 jets. In mid-1951, the more powerful MiG-15bis began to replace the basic MiG-15 in Korea, offering a small, but significant, improvement in thrust. When the USAF switched its B-29s to night attacks, the aircraft proved almost invulnerable, and the ageing La-11s used as nightfighters could not stop the raiders. The 64th IAK's night-fighter unit, the 351st IAP, therefore re-equipped one of its two squadrons with MiGs during February 1952, the other retaining La-11s.

Within a year the unit had provided an ace, Anatoli Karelin, whose five kills (one scored in the La-11) won him the award of a Hero of the Soviet Union. The night sky was a dangerous place for the single-seat, radarless, MiG, which had to contend with prowling Allied nightfighters (all with radar). The MiG-15 had to get closer to its target than it would have done by day, and this exposed it to hostile fire. As an example, Karelin's fifth victim, a B-29, put 117 holes in his jet and severed its fuel supply line.

The third Division to join the fray was the 304th IAD, which deployed to Tapao when it was complete. The replacement unit for the 324th IAD was a PVO unit, the 97th IAD. This outfit proved so ill-prepared that in

April 1952 it had to be withdrawn to the second line after only two months of combat, and the 196th IAP briefly re-entered the fray, while the replacement unit underwent further training. Other MiG units operating in Korea included the 535th IAP and the 878th IAP.

Soviet tactics differed little from those used in the closing stages of the Great Patriotic War. The basic unit remained the *Para* (pair) or *Zveno* (four aircraft section), although an early reliance on formations of eight (two *zvenos*) was replaced by use of more flexible six-jet formations late in the war. Squadrons operated in shifts, going from one state of readiness to the next every two hours. GCI radar controllers would scramble the unit, who would then keep the pilots appraised of the enemy's approach.

The GCI alert system avoided maintaining pilots at cockpit readiness wherever possible, since they would become exhausted in the hot, damp, summer weather, or cold and fatigued in winter. The cramped dimensions of the MiG-15's cockpit made it impossible for pilots to wear thick, warm, fur-lined clothing, and so, in winter as in summer, the unfortunate pilots on alert had to sit in lightweight flying kit, with only a thin leather jacket to ward off the bitter cold. In summer they sweltered, since there was no cockpit air conditioning, and there were no air ventilated suits.

MiGs would loiter above the target they were defending, in two layers, with the upper 'cover' layer intended to move against any escorts with the advantages of speed and height, while the lower 'attack' layer would move against the fighter-bombers. The unit would also have a reserve group, ready to offer support whenever needed. Favourite tactics included hit and run attacks from altitude, pairs diving down for a slash attack before using their energy to climb to safety. Against fighter-bombers, however, some experienced pilots favoured surprise attacks from underneath, exploiting the terrain to approach the enemy undetected.

APPENDICES

Ascertaining the exact number of kills scored by UN pilots in the Korean War is probably impossible. In addition to the problems posed by too loose criteria for awarding 'kills', the total number of enemy aircraft destroyed has progressively been reduced since the war, and the number of admitted air-to-air losses has steadily risen. An air-to-air kill:loss ratio which appeared to be in the order of 10:1 after the war now appears closer to 2:1. Of USAF victory claims recognised at the time, only some were eventually awarded as credits in the aftermath of the war, thus producing a considerable shortfall in the final wartime totals – it has never officially been revealed which claims failed to become credits. Therefore, the numbers of kills listed for USAF pilots in this appendix represent claims, not credits.

The breakdown of claims revealed the MiG-15 as the most frequent opponent (841 claims, plus a single unidentified jet, probably misidentified as a Yak-15 at the time), followed by the Yak-9 (14 claims, plus four Yak-3s), the Il-10 (nine claims, plus an Il-12), the Tupolev Tu-2 (nine claims), the Lavochkin La-9 (six claims, plus three La-7s) and with single claims for the Po-2 and Yak-18.

The bulk of victories claimed came from F-86 Sabre pilots, and of these 818 kills, a massive 305.5 were credited at the time to the 39 top-scoring pilots (all aces), with another 292 being claimed by the 115 pilots who downed two or more kills. While all the true aces (those who had five or more victory claims) are listed in the following tables, it is not possible in a book of this size to list every Sabre pilot who claimed an enemy aircraft.

Instead, the top-scoring pilots from each Sabre unit are listed, together with any interesting pilots (those with victories from World War 2, or on exchange from the USN, USMC or Commonwealth air forces, for example). We have also attempted to list all of the pilots who claimed kills while flying other aircraft types.

We have not, however, included radar operators or gunners. Of these other USAF types, B-29s accounted for 27 claims, F-80s for 17, F-51Ds for 12, F-84s for 10, F-94s for four and F-82s for three, with a B-26 claiming a solitary victory.

US Air Force

FIGHTER UNITS

4th Fighter Intercept Group/Wing*

4TH FIG STAFF (20.5 claims)
4TH FIW STAFF (4 claims)

Lt Col Glenn T Eagleston	2 kills (plus 18.5 WW 2)
Maj Franklin L Fisher	3 kills
Col Frances S Gabreski	2 kills (of 6.5 total)
Lt Col William J Hovde	1 kill (plus 10.5 WW 2)
Lt Col George L Jones	1.5 kills (of 6.5 total)
Col John C Meyer	2 kills (plus 24 WW 2)
Col Benjamin S Preston	4 kills
Lt Cdr Paul E Pugh (USN)	2 kills
Col Harrison R Thyng	3 kills (of 5 total)

334th FIS (142.5 claims)

Maj Felix Asla	1 kill (of 4 total
Capt Richard S Becker	5 kills
Maj Frederick C Blesse	10 kills
1 Lt Charles G Cleveland	4 kills
Lt Colonel William G Cosby	2 kills (of 3 total)
Maj George A Davis	14 kills
Capt Manuel J Fernandez	14.5 kills
Flt Lt Ernie Glover (RCAF)	3 kills
Maj James P Hagerstrom	1 kill (of 8.5 total)
Maj James Jabara	15 kills
Flt Lt J A O Levesque (RCAF)	1 kill
Capt Leonard W Lilley	7 kills
Capt Ralph S Parr	10 kills
Lt Col James B Raebel	1 kill (of 3 total)
Maj Foster L Smith	1 kill (of 4.5 total)
Maj William T Whisner	2 kills (of 5.5 total)

335TH FIS (218.5 claims)

Maj Zane S Amell	3 kills
Col Royal N Baker	9 kills (of 13 total)
1 Lt Richard S Becker	5 kills
Capt Philip E Colman	4 kills (plus 5 WW 2)
Capt Clyde A Curtin	5 kills
Capt Carl K Dittmer	3 kills
1 Lt Billy B Dobbs	4 kills
Capt Doug F Durnford (USMC)	0.5 kill
Lt Col Vermont Garrison	10 kills
Capt Ralph D Gibson	5 kills
Maj Alex J Gillis (USMC)	3 kills
Maj James P Hagerstrom	1 kill (of 8.5 total)
Col James K Johnson	10 kills
Capt Clifford D Jolley	7 kills
Lt Col George L Jones	3 kills (of 6.5 total)
1 Lt James H Kasler	6 kills

Capt Robert T Latshaw, Jr	5 kills
Capt Robert J Love	6 kills
1 Lt James F Low	9 kills
Maj Winton W Marshall	6.5 kills
Maj Jack E Mass	4 kills
Capt Conrad E Mattson	4 kills (plus 1 WW 2)
Capt Lonnie R Moore	10 kills
Capt Milton E Nelson	4 kills
Flt Lt J M Nicholls (RAF)	2 kills
1 Lt.Ira M.Porter	3 kills
1 Lt Merton E Ricker	3 kills
1 Lt Albert B Smiley	3 kills
Maj Foster L Smith	3.5 kills (of 4.5 total)
Col Harrison R Thyng	2 kills (of 5 total)
Capt Murray A Winslow	4 kills
Lt Col Benjamin H Emmert, Jr	1 kill (plus 6 WW 2)

336TH FIS (116.5 claims)

Maj Felix Asla	3 kills (of 4 total)
Col Royal V Baker	4 kills (of 13 total)
Capt Ralph E Banks	4 kills
Maj Stephen L Bettinger	5 kills
Maj William L Cosby	1 kill (of 3 total)
Maj Richard D Creighton	5 kills
Lt Simpson Evans, Jr (USN)	1 kill
1 Lt Walter W Fellman	4 kills
Capt Peter J Frederick	3 kills
Lt Col Louis A Green	4 kills
Capt William F Guss (USMC)	1 kill
Lt Col Bruce H Hinton	2 kills
Flt Lt Graham S Hulse (RAF)	3 kills
1 Lt Anthony Kulengosky	1 kill (of 3 total)
Capt Brooks J Liles	4 kills
Capt Robert H Moore	5 kills
Maj Charles D Owens	2 kills
Lt Col J S Payne (USMC)	1 kill
Maj Robinson Risner	8 kills
Maj Thomas M Sellers (USMC)	2 kills
Capt Houston N Tuel	3 kills

* The 4th FIG/4th FIW accounted for 54 per cent of USAF victory claims in Korea

51st Fighter Intercept Group/Wing

51ST FIG STAFF (5 claims)
51ST FIW STAFF (6.5 claims)

Col Francis S Gabreski	4.5 kills (of 6.5 total)
Lt Col George L Jones	2 kills (of 6.5 total)
Col Walker M Mahurin	1 kill (of 3.5 total)
Flt Lt Lawrence E Spurr (RCAF)	1 kill
Maj William H Wescott	1 kill (of 5 total)

16TH FIS (85 claims)

Maj Donald E Adams	6.5 kills
1 Lt Edwin E Aldrin	2 kills
Col Robert P Baldwin	1 kill (of 5 total)
Capt Cecil G Foster	9 kills
Lt Col Edwin Heller	3.5 kills (plus 5.5 WW 2
Capt Vincent Marzelo (USMC)	1 kill

1 Lt James A McCulley	3 kills
Capt Dolphin D Overton	5 kills
1 Lt Robert L Sands	3 kills
Capt Richard H Schoenemann	3 kills
Maj William F Sheaffer	3 kills
Capt Robert Wade (USMC)	1 kill

25TH FIS (110.5 claims)

Col Robert P Baldwin	3 kills (of 5 total)
Capt Norman L Box	3 kills
1 Lt Henry Buttelmann	7 kills
Maj Van E Chandler	3 kills (plus 7 WW 2)
Flt Lt R T F Dickinson (RAF)	1 kill
Maj John Glenn, Jr (USMC)	3 kills
Maj Elmer W Harris	3 kills (plus 3 strafe)
Capt H Jensen (USMC)	1 kill
Capt Iven C Kincheloe	9 kills
1 Lt Anthony Kulengosky	2 kills (of 3 total)
Flt Lt J H J Lovell (RAF)	1 kill
Col Walker M Mahurin	2.5 kills (of 3.5 total)
Lt Col James B Raebel	2 kills (of 3 total)
Maj William H Wescott	4 kills (of 5 total)
Maj William T Whisner	3.5 kills (of 5.5 total)
Maj Herman W Visscher	1 kill (plus 5 WW 2)

39TH FIS (101 claims)

Col Robert P Baldwin	1 kill (of 5 total)
Maj John Bolt (USMC)	6 kills
Maj Lowell K Brueland	2 kills (plus 12.5 WW 2)
Capt Harold E Fischer	10 kills
Flt Lt John H Granville-White (RAF)	1 kill
Maj John J Hockery	1 kill (plus 7 WW 2)
1 Lt Francis A Humphreys	3 kills
Flt Lt Claude A LaFrance (RCAF)	1 kill
Sqn Ldr James D Lindsay (RCAF)	2 kills
Col John W Mitchell	4 kills (plus 11 WW 2)
Capt Joseph M McConnell	16 kills
Lt Col George I Ruddell	8 kills

68TH F(AW)S (2 claims)

1 Lt William G Hudson	1 kill
1 Lt Charles B Moran	1 kill

319TH FIS (4 claims)

Capt Benjamin L Fithian	1 kill
Lt Col Robert V McHale	1 kill
Capt John R Phillips	1 kill
2 Lt Stanton G Wilcox	1 kill (ramming)

339TH F(AW)S (1 claim)

Maj James W Little	1 kill

Fighter-Bomber Units

8TH FBS

2 Lt Orrin R Fox	2 kills (F-51)
1 Lt Roy W Marsh	1 kill (F-80)
1 Lt Harry T Sandlin	1 kill (F-51)

9TH FBS

Capt Kenneth L Skeen	1 kill (F-84)

12TH FBS

1 Lt Donald R Forbes	1 kill (F-86)
1 Lt James L Glessner	1 kill (F-51)

16TH FBS

1 Lt Russell Brown	1 kill (F-80)
1 Lt William W McAllister	1 kill (F-80)

27TH FEG

Lt Col William E Bertram	1 kill (F-84)

35TH FBS

1 Lt Richard J Burns	1 kill (F-51)
Capt Francis Clark	1 kill (F-80)
1 Lt Robert H Dewald	1 kill (F-80)
2 Lt David H Goodnough	1 kill (F-80)
Capt Raymond E Schilleref	1 kill (F-80)
1 Lt Robert E Wayne	2 kills (F-80)

36TH FBS

2 Lt Elwood A Kees	1 kill (F-80)
1 Lt Howard J Landry	1 kill (F-80)
Capt Robert L Lee	1 kill (F-80)
1 Lt Robert D McKee	1 kill (F-80)
2 Lt Robert E Smith	1 kill (F-80)
1 Lt John B Thomas	1 kill (F-80)
1 Lt Charles A Wurster	2 kills (F-80)

67TH FBS

Capt Elmer N Dunlap	0.5 kill (F-86)
Maj Howard Ebersole	1 kill (F-86)
Capt Alma R Flake	kills (F-51)
Maj James P Hagerstrom	6.5 kills (8.5 total/F-86)
1 Lt James B Harrison	1 kill (F-51)
Col Maurice L Martin	1 kill (F-86)
1 Lt John L Metten	1 kill (F-86)
Maj Arnold Mullins	1 kill (F-51)
Capt Howard I Price	1.5 kill (F-51)
1 Lt Henry S Reynolds	0.5 kill (F-51)
Capt Robert D Thresher	1 kill (F-51)

111TH FBS

1 Lt Kenneth C Cooley	1 kill (F-84)
1 Lt John M Hewett, Jr	0.5 kill (F-84)

154TH FBS

1 Lt Farrie D Fortner	1 kill (F-84)

158TH FBS

Capt Paul C Mitchell	1 kill (F-84)

182ND FBS

Lt Arthur E Oligher	0.5 kill (F-84)
Capt Harry L Underwood	0.5 kill (F-84)

522ND FES

Capt William W Slaughter	1 kill (F-84)

523RD FES

1 Lt Jacob Kratt Jr	3 kills (F-84)

Bomber Units*

8TH BS

Capt Richard M Heyman	1 kill (B-26)

* 27 kills were made by B-29 gunners, but these fall outside the scope of this appendix.

US Navy*

VC-3

Lt Guy Bordelon	five kills (F4U-5N)

VF-51

Ens E W Brown	one kill (F9F-2)
Lt Leonard Plog	one kill (F9F-2)

VF-111

Lt Cdr W T Amen	one kill (F9F-2)
Lt Cdr W E Lamb	one kill (F9F-2) (plus 5 WW 2)
Lt R E Parker	one kill (F9F-2)
Ens F C Weber	one kill (F9F-2)

VF-781

Lt(jg) J D Middleton	onc kill (F9F-2)
Lt E R Williams	one kill (F9F-2)

* US Navy pilots flying with USAF Sabre units scored three more victories. This brought the kill tally to 16.

US Marine Corps*

VMA-312

Lt Jesse Folmar	one kill (FG-1D/F4U-4)

VMC-1

Maj George Linnemeier	one kill (AD4)

VMF(N)-513

Lt John Andre	one kill (F4U-5N)
Lt Col Robert Conley	one kill (F3D)
Lt Joseph Corvi	one kill (F3D)
1st Lt H Daigh	one kill (F4U-5N)
Capt Oliver Davis	one kill (F3D)
Capt Philip De Long	one kill (F4U-5N)
Maj Elswin Dunn	one kill (F3D)
Capt Donald Fenton	one kill (F4U-5N)
Maj Eugene Van Grundy	one kill (F7F-3N)
Capt E B Long	one kill (F7F-3N)
Maj William Stratton	one kill (F3D)
Capt J Weaver	one kill (F3D)

*Pilots flying with the 4th and 51st FIWs scored 21.5 kills, and one more Marine (Lt W M Schirra) scored a kill while flying F-84s. This brought total claims to 35.5

F-86E-5-NA (side view and plan forms)

F-86F wing (with fence)

**North American F-86 Sabre
1/72nd scale**

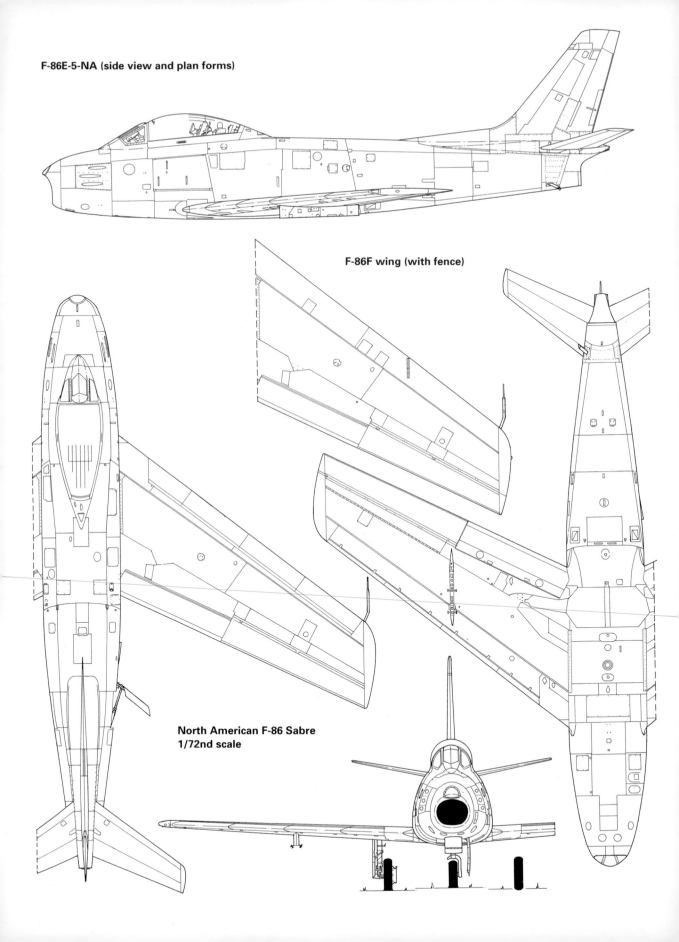

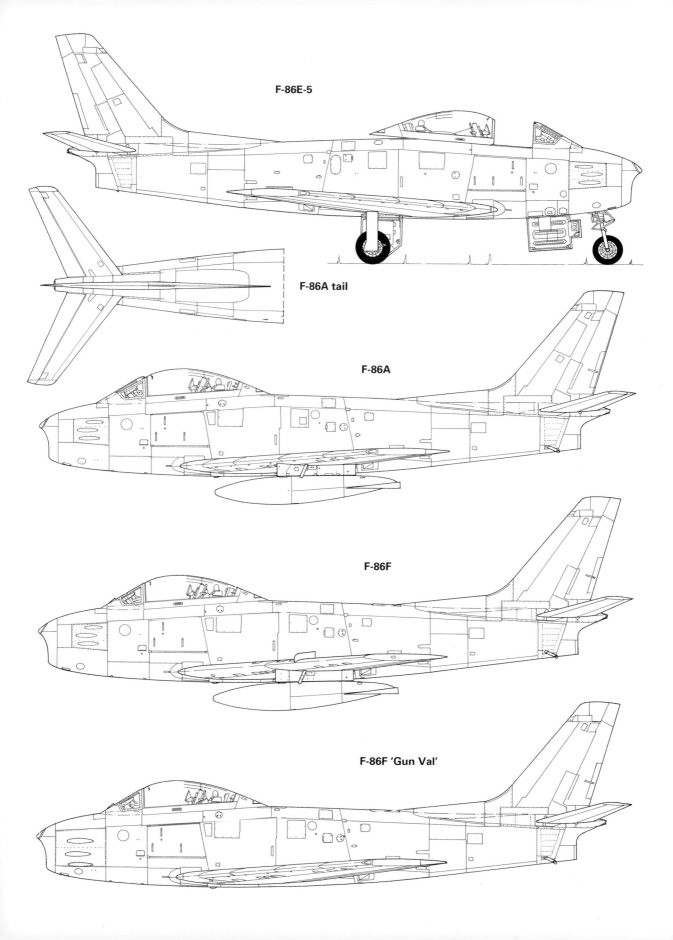

F-86E-5

F-86A tail

F-86A

F-86F

F-86F 'Gun Val'

COLOUR PLATES

1
F-86E-1-NA 50-623 *Pretty Mary & the Js*, flown by Col Harrison R Thyng, CO 4th FIW
A seasoned fighter pilot from World War 2, with kills against the Japanese and the Luftwaffe, Thyng had commanded a P-47N squadron in the Far East in 1944/45. He attained ace status (becoming the War's 16th ace) shortly before handing over the 4th FIW to Col James Johnson. Two of his five kills were officially credited while he was flying with the 335th FIS.

2
F-86E-10-NA 51-2747 *HONEST JOHN*, flown by Col Walker M 'Bud' Mahurin, CO 4th FIG
Mahurin was another highly experienced fighter pilot, having scored 21 kills against the Luftwaffe in World War 2. The first of his 3.5 victory claims was with the 51st FIW, the others being made under the auspices of the 25th FIS. This aircraft, however, was flown by Mahurin during his tenure as commander of the 4th FIG.

3
F-86F-10-NA 51-12941, flown by Col James K Johnson, CO 4th FIW
Johnson took over the 4th from Thyng and flew this anonymous, but highly polished, F-86F. It was decorated only with the badge of the 335th FIS and yellow ID bands on the wings, fuselage and, uniquely to the 4th, the tailfin as well. Johnson believed strongly in leading from the front, and duly became a one of the first double aces in Korea, scoring exactly ten kills

4
F-86A-5-NA 49-1281, flown by Col Glenn T Eagleston, CO 334th FIS/ 4th FIW
As commander of the 334th FIS, Eagleston added three MiGs to his wartime tally of 18.5. His jet wears the original identity stripes adopted by the 4th before black-edged yellow bands took over. Intake lips were sometimes painted in the squadron colour also.

5
F-86A-5-NA 48-259, flown by Capt (later Maj) James Jabara, 334th FIS/4th FIW
In his two tours in Korea, Jabara achieved a great deal. Claiming his fifth and sixth kills on 20 May 1951, he became the first 'ace' of the conflict, scoring these victories in a jet with one hung drop tank! He used a string of aircraft on his way to scoring 15 victories, but his own personal jet on his first tour was 48-259.

6
F-86F-1-NA 51-2857, flown by Capt Manuel J 'Pete' Fernandez, Jr, 334th FIS/4th FIW
This aircraft was often used by Jabara during his second tour, despite being assigned to one of the 334th FIS's other major aces, Capt 'Pete' Fernandez. The latter overtook Royal Baker as the leading scorer in May 1953, and was he himself overtaken by McConnell.

7
F-86E-10-NA 51-2821, flown by Maj Frederick C 'Boots' Blesse, 334th FIS/4th FIW
Despite his score of ten kills, Frederick Blesse's major contribution to air combat history was his treatise, *No Guts, No Glory*, a volume which had a major influence a decade later when fighter tactics in Vietnam were shaken up to reflect his ideas.

8
F-86F-30-NA 52-4778 *Barb/Vent De Mort*, flown by Capt Ralph S Parr, 334th FIS/4th FIW
Parr flew a 185-mission tour with the 7th FBS during 1950-51, then returned to Korea in 1953 to become a double ace on the F-86! He was assigned a variety of aircraft, including 52-4778 *Barb/Vent de Morte* seen here, as well as 51-12955 *Barbara* and 51-12959.

9
F-86E-10-NA 51-2764, flown by Capt Leonard W Lilley, 334th FIS/4th FIW
The USAF's 22nd ace, Lilley finished the war with seven kills, several of which were scored in this conservatively marked F-86E

10
F-86A-5-NA 49-1184 *Miss Behaving*, flown by 1st Lt Richard S Becker, 334th FIS/4th FIW
Dick Becker flew a number of F-86As to amass his score of five aircraft, all of them striped F-86As like his officially assigned *Miss Behaving*. A black stripe was also applied to the leading edge of the rudder, as well as to the fuselage and wings.

11
F-86F-10-NA 51-12953, flown by Lt Col Vermont Garrison, CO 335th FIS/4th FIW
Jet ace No 32, and a double ace by the time his tour of duty had ended, Garrison was, at 37, one of the oldest of the elite. His experience and skill led to his appointment to the Project *Gunval* Sabre team. These aircraft were not painted up in full unit markings, unlike his own F-86F, seen here.

12
F-86F-10-NA 51-12972 *Billie*, flown by Capt Lonnie R Moore, 335th FIS/4th FIW
Lonnie Moore's own F-86F wore the name *Billie* on the port side, with *Margie* to starboard behind the gun muzzle blast panel. Like Garrison, he was one of the *Gunval* pilots, but it is not certain whether any of the kills he scored whilst assigned to the project were among his final claims.

13
F-86E-10-NA 51-2834 *Jolley Roger*, flown by Capt Clifford D Jolley, 335th FIS/4th FIW
Jolley, 18th ace of the war, was one of the pilots chosen for the evaluation of six factory-fresh F-

86Fs fitted with solid fuel rocket motors in the tail, below the jet pipe. These modified jets initially proved successful with their extra thrust for higher acceleration, Jolley scoring two of his seven victories using the rocket-equipped aircraft. Handling problems were severe, however, and one of the evaluation pilots was killed in combat. The aircraft shown here was Jolley's own F-86E, and it was eventually reassigned to 'Jolting' Joe Romack and renamed *Patricia II*, but retained Jolley's distinctive skull-and-crossbones flag.

14

F-86E-10-NA 51-2769 *BERNIE'S BO*, flown by Capt Robert J Love, 335th FIS/4th FIW
Bernie's Bo was the mount of Bob Love, who ended the war with six kills. The 335th FIS was the top-scoring unit of the war with 218.5 victories.

15

F-86F-30-NA 52-4416 *Boomer*, flown by Capt Clyde A Curtin, 335th FIS/4th FIW
Curtin flew this slatted F-86F during the summer of 1952. The 335th owed its high score to the consistency of its aircrew, rather than to the efforts of a handful of 'star pilots'.

16

F-86A-5-NA 48-261, flown by 1st Lt Donald Torres, 335th FIS/4th FIW
Camouflaged Sabres were a rarity in Korea, although Russian veterans often recall their opponents as having flown painted aircraft. This faded and patched olive drab F-86A was assigned to 1st Lt Donald Torres

17

F-86E-10-NA 51-2822 *THE KING/Angel Face & The Babes*, flown by Col Royal V 'The King' Baker, 336th FIS/4th FIW
For months the leading scorer in Korea, Col Baker ended the war with 13 kills – 12 MiGs and a single La-9. This left him fourth on the list of top-scorers.

18

F-86E-10-NA 51-2824 *Little Mike/Ohio Mike*, flown by Capt (later Maj) Robinson Risner, 336th FIS/4th FIW
Risner ended his tour with eight victories, placing him 12th on the list of top-scoring pilots in Korea. His aircraft carried a massive rendition of a cartoon rabbit, wearing a deerstalker and checking a discharge paper with a large magnifying glass, on both sides of the fuselage, making it one of the most colourful aircraft in the wing.

19

F-86A-5-NA 49-1225, flown by Maj Richard D Creighton, 336th FIS/4th FIW
One of the 336th FIS's earliest aces was Richard Creighton, a jet pioneer who had set a speed record in the F-86 and who had been at the forefront of the development of jet fighter tactics prior to the Korean War.

20

F-86E-10-NA 51-2767 *THE CHOPPER*, flown by Maj Felix Asla, Jr, 336th FIS/4th FIW

During the summer of 1952 the 336th FIS included a number of sharkmouthed F-86s, the aircraft of Felix Asla, Jr, being one of the more restrained. Asla ended the war with four kills (despite the eight red stars on his aircraft!), scoring the first of these while serving with the 334th FIS.

21

F-86E-10-NA 51-2800 *EL DIABLO*, flown by Capt (later Maj) Charles D 'Chuck' Owens, 336th FIS/4th FIW
This optimistic scoreboard successfully hides the fact that Owens was officially credited with just two victories. The large number of truck symbols, together with the tank, might indicate that he threw his efforts into ground strafing, a practise which became common even before the conversion of two fighter bomber wings to the F-86.

22

F-86A-5-NA 49-1175 *PAUL'S MIG KILLER*, flown by 1st Lt Joseph E Fields, 336th FIS/4th FIW
Joe Fields flew an even more gaudily decorated aircraft than Chuck Owens, with a winning combination of squadron badge and massive sharkmouth – the latter was perhaps the largest in use on a Sabre in Korea. Sharkmouths had been popular on F-80s and F-51s early in the war, but were removed in deference to local sensibilities, with a fear that pilots of aircraft which crash-landed wearing such 'devilish' markings might receive an unfriendly reception.

23

F-86E-10-NA 51-2740 *GABBY*, flown by Col Francis S Gabreski, CO 51st FIW
Col Francis Gabreski led the 51st with verve and drive, but not always with a strict adherence to the rules. He instituted *Maple Special* missions for example, which were unauthorised hot pursuits into Manchuria. These were kept secret from the brass at Suwon and only the most experienced pilots were in on the secret. Gabreski's own F-86 carried his nickname, underlined by a smoking cigar. He also scored some of his 6.5 kills in Wescott's *Lady Frances*.

24

F-86F-10-NA 51-12950 Mitch's Squitch, flown by Col John W Mitchell, CO 51st FIW
Although it wore the yellow tail stripe of the 39th FIS, Mitchell's F-86 had thin red, yellow and blue nose bands signifying the three squadron's under his command. He added four victories to the 11 he'd amassed in World War 2.

25

F-86E-10-NA 51-2756 *HELL-ER BUST X*, flown by Maj (later Lt Col) Edwin L Heller, 16th FIS/51st FIW
A veteran Eighth Air Force ace during World war 2, Heller flew a succession of F-86s, all named *Hell-er Bust*. A controversial leader, Heller pushed the rules whenever possible, and paid scant regard to the restrictions concerning going north of the Yalu.

26

F-86E-10-NA 51-2738 *FOUR KINGS & A QUEEN*, flown by 1st Lt (later Capt) Cecil Foster, 16th

FIS/51st FIW

A nine-victory ace, Foster flew this F-86E, which he named *Three Kings*, later renaming her *Four Kings and a Queen* after the birth of his fourth son. The 16th FIS was the least successful long-term Sabre squadron in Korea, scoring only 85 victories.

27

F-86E-1-NA 50-631 *DOLPH'S DEVIL,* flown by Capt Dolphin D Overton III, 16th FIS/51st FIW

Dolph Overton just made it onto the official list of aces, downing five aircraft (all MiG-15s) in four successive days in January 1953, as he reached the end of his tour – he had previously completed 102 missions in F-84s with the 8th FBS/49th FBW.

28

F-86E-10-NA 51-2731 *IVAN,* flown by 1st Lt (later Capt) Iven Kincheloe, 25th FIS/51st FIW

Later a famous test pilot, Kincheloe bowed to the inevitable and spelt his aircraft's name in the conventional way with an 'a'. He scored five aerial victories (with three more ground kills), bringing him the coveted status of 'ace'.

29

F-86F-1-NA 51-2890, flown by 1st Lt Henry 'Hank' Buttlemann, 25th FIS/51st FIW

Only a handful of Sabres in Korea received the new-fangled 'US AIR FORCE' legend on the nose before the war ended. Officially introduced on new production aircraft in June 1953, its application to in-service aircraft took months to complete. At 23, Buttelmann was the youngest ace in Korea, scoring seven kills.

30

F-86E-10-NA 51-2735 *Elenore E,* flown by Maj William T Whisner, 25th FIS/51st FIW

William Whisner's 5.5 kills added to his tally of five German aircraft dispatched in World War 2. His aircraft lacked the checkerboard fin decoration applied later to virtually all 51st FIW Sabres. The 25th FIS was the most successful of the 51st's three squadrons, scoring 110.5 victories.

31

F-86E-10-NA 51-2746 LADY FRANCES/MICHIGAN CENTER, flown by Maj William Wescott, 25th FIS/51st FIW

Wescott's *LADY FRANCES* was used by Gabreski to score one of his victories, but also served as the mount for several of Wescott's five kills – the Sabre also bore the legend *MICHIGAN CENTER* to starboard.

32

F-86F-30-NA 52-4584 *MIG MAD MARINE/LYN ANNIE DAVE I,* flown by Maj John Glenn, USMC, 25th FIS/51st FIW

The 25th FIS included a number of exchange pilots, none of them more famous than John Glenn. There have been suggestions that such exchange tours were deliberately managed to prevent the officers concerned from gaining five kills, the USAF preferring its own pilots to get the glory, though this cannot be confirmed. Glenn scored three kills in the Sabre, justifying the aircraft's

huge and gaudy nickname – these kills never appeared in the USAF's official records, however.

33

F-86E-1-NA 50-649 *AUNT MYRNA,* flown by Lt Walter Copeland, 25th FIS/51st FIW

Copeland scored a single victory in his *Aunt Myrna*, contributing to the 25th FIS's wartime total of 110.5 kills. Apart from being the top-scoring unit in the wing, the 25th FIS actually claimed the last MiG to be shot down in the Korean War, this aircraft falling before the guns of 2nd Lt Sam Young.

34

F-86F-1-NA 51-2910 *BEAUTIOUS BUTCH II* flown by 1st Lt Joseph M McConnell, 39th FIS/51st FIW

UN 'ace of aces', and bettered only by a pair of Russian MiG-15 pilots, McConnell streaked past rivals Jabara and Fernandez to take the lead in the 5th Air Force MiG race. He flew a string of Sabres, including at least three named *Beautious Butch*. The last was 51-2910, which had the diving red MiG silhouette kill markings replaced by red stars when the jet was repainted after his 16th kill for PR purposes. The spelling of the name was changed to *Beauteous Butch II* at the same time.

35

F-86F-10-NA Sabre 51-12958 *the PAPER TIGER,* flown by 1st Lt (later Capt) Harold E Fischer, 39th FIS/51st FIW

Harold Fischer came to the F-86 after a tour on F-84s. He rapidly became a highly-skilled operator, becoming the 25th jet ace of the war, having scored 10 kills by the time he was shot down over China in April 1953. His aircraft wears the same 'diving MiG' kill markings as McConnell's, and is decorated with the sharkmouth usually associated with the *Tiger Flight* of the 25th FIS.

36

F-86F-10-NA 51-12940 *MIG MAD MAVIS,* flown by Lt Col George I Ruddell, CO 39th FIS/51st FIW

With triple 'command stripes' across the nose, *MIG MAD MAVIS* was the mount of the commanding officer of the 39th FIS, Lt Col George Ruddell. He scored an eventual eight kills and proved a popular and effective commander.

37

F-86F-1-NA 51-2852 *DARLING DOTTIE,* flown by Maj John F Bolt, USMC, 39th FIS/51st FIW

John Bolt was an 89-mission veteran Panther pilot with VMF-115 'Able Eagles' when he was chosen as one of several aircrew from the unit to serve with the 39th FIS during the Korean War. Flying this plain F-86F, he was able to become the only Marine ace of the conflict, adding six kills to his World War 2 total of six.

38

F-86F-1-NA 51-2897 THE HUFF, flown by Lt James L Thompson, 39th FIS/51st FIW

Perhaps the most colourfully marked Sabre of the war was Lt Jim Thompson's *The Huff*, whose dragon motif was reportedly inspired by a similar decoration spotted on a particularly well-flown enemy MiG-15. His personal score was a pair of MiG-15s, downed in May and June of 1953.

39

F-82G-NA 46-383, flown by Lt William 'Skeeter' Hudson, with Lt Carl Fraser, 68th F(AW)S

Whilst performing a daylight CAP over Kimpo on 27 June 1950 with three other F-82Gs, the crew of -383 were bounced by a flight of North Korean Yaks. Hudson and Fraser quickly turned the tables, despatching a grey-painted Yak-7U (apparently coded C6),whose pilot bailed out, but whose back-seater did not attempt to escape.

40

F-94B-5-LO 51-5449, flown by Capt Ben Fithian, with Lt Sam R Lyons, 319th FIS

Four enemy aircraft fell to the F-94, though one of these victories was somewhat pyhrric – a Po-2 was downed when the F-94 pursuing it simply flew straight through the lightweight biplane, destroying both aircraft and killing both crews.

41

F-51D-30-NT 45-11736, flown by Lt James Glessner, 12th FBS/18th FBG

The 12th FBS applied sharkmouths to its aircraft, including this machine, flown by Lt James Glessner when he scored his Yak-9 kill on 2 November 1950.

42

F-51D-30-NA 44-75728, flown by Maj Arnold 'Moon' Mullins, 67th FBS/18th FBG

With four stars below the windscreen indicating the destruction of four aircraft (one in the air, three on the ground), this is Maj Arnold Mullins' personal F-51D.

43

F-86F-30-NA 52-4341 *MIG POISON*, flown by Maj James P Hagerstrom, 67th FBS/18th FBG

When the 18th FBG converted from the F-51D Mustang to the F-86F, several experienced pilots from the 4th and 51st FIWs were transferred in to help with jet conversion. One of these was Maj Hagerstrom, who added 6.5 kills to the two he'd amassed with the 4th FIW. The red intake lip was typical of 18th FBW Sabres.

44

F-84E-25-RE 51-493, flown by Lt Jacob Kratt, Jr, 523rd FES/27th FEW

The 27th FEW was a SAC unit tasked with long range escort, but was deployed to Korea, with its F-84Es, to operate in the less familiar close air support role. Several F-84 pilots scored air-to-air victories, but Kratt was the most successful, downing a pair of MiG-15s and a single piston-engined Yak.

45

B-29B-60-BA 44-84057 *COMMAND DECISION*, 28th BS/19th BG (Medium), Kadena, Okinawa

The B-29 was claimed to be the second-highest scoring UN aircraft of the Korean War after the Sabre, and the gunners of this aircraft actually amassed a total of five MiG credits, making the aircraft an ace! Sgt Billy Beach claimed two, with Technical Sergeants Norman Greene and Charles Summers claiming another two between them, and Staff Sergeant Michael Martocchia claiming the fifth. *Command Decision* was typical of B-29s operating over Korea, with hastily applied black undersides obscuring much of the USAF legend on the forward fuselage. The aircraft carried its name, and nose art featuring two of Disney's seven dwarves, on the starboard side of the nose.

46

F4U-5N 24453 *ANNIE MO*, flown by Lt Guy 'Lucky Pierre' Bordelon, 'Detachment Dog', VC-3, detached ashore to K-6 from USS *Princeton*

Bordelon was the only non-Sabre ace of the war, and truly lived up to his nickname of 'Lucky Pierre'. Of all the hopeful (and experienced) US Navy F4U-5N pilots, Bordelon got the lucky break which saw him detached ashore with two aircraft specifically to hunt nocturnal 'Bedcheck Charlie' raiders. All the white markings on Bordelon's glossy midnight blue Corsair were faintly oversprayed to reduce their conspicuity.

47

F9F-2 (BuNo unknown), flown by Lt Leonard Plog, VF-51, USS *Valley Forge*

The Navy allowed the application of small victory and mission markings, but did not allow the use of individual aircraft names or nose art, and with few exceptions, the rules were not broken. Units were permitted to apply small patches of colour on the noses, engine cowls and/or fuel tanks of their aircraft, but not all did. Thus the aircraft flown by Leonard Plog (and wingman Ens E W Brown) to score their Yak kills on 3 July 1950.

48

F9F-2 (BuNo unknown), flown by Lt(jg) J D Middleton, VF-781, USS *Oriskany*

After an unusual action on 18 November 1952, Middleton and his wingman, Lt E R Williams were credited with two MiG-kills, while Lt(jg) D M Rowlands damaged a third. This incident was initially hushed up by the Navy, as the enemy aircraft had been Russian MiG-15s (not nominally North Korean) operating from a base near Vladivostock.

49

FG-1D (F4U-4) (BuNo 92701), flown by Capt Jesse Folmar, VMA-312

Folmar was able to down one of a pair of MiG-15s which attacked him and his wingman on 10 September 1952, but was himself shot down when attacked by four more MiGs. His F4U (which he was not flying when he was shot down) was decorated with the silhouette of a diving MiG-15.

50

F4U-5N (BuNo 123180), flown by Capt John Andre, VMF(N)-513

John Andre's 7 June 1952 kill made him an ace, since it added to his four kills scored during World War 2.

51

F7F-3N (BuNo unknown), flown by Capt E B Long with WO R C Buckingham, VMF(N)-513

Tigercats were primarily used for night interdiction

duties, but also mounted night CAPs in an effort to prevent nuisance attacks by 'Bedcheck Charlies'. Long scored the first USMC night kill of the war (and the Tigercats first victory ever) on 1 July 1951, shooting down a Po-2 near Kimpo.

52
F3D-2 (BuNo unknown), flown by Maj William Stratton with MSgt Hans Hoglind, VMF(N)-513
Although it was not introduced until 1952, the Skyknight proved very successful, downing seven aircraft, including six MiG-15s. This success was largely due to the jet's three radar sets: AN/APG-26 for gun ranging and lock-on; AN/APS-21 for search out to 15 miles; and the four-mile range AN/APS-28 tail warning radar. The first of the Skynight's kills was scored by Bill Stratton on 2 November 1952.

53
Sea Fury FB.Mk 11, flown by Lt Peter 'Hoagy' Carmichael, No 802 Sqn, HMS *Ocean*
Carmichael's 9 August 1952 kill was the first MiG-15 to fall to a piston-engined fighter, and was the only confirmed kill by a British pilot flying a British aircraft achieved in Korea.

54
Meteor F.Mk 8 A77-17 *BOWL 'EM OVER!*, flown by Flg Off Bruce Gogerly, No 77 Sqn,
BOWL 'EM OVER was Gogerly's aircraft, but was not used by him for his epic MiG-15 kill on 1 December 1951 – he was actually flying WO Bob Turner's A77-15, nicknamed *Elyana*, on this occasion. The second Meteor kill was made on 8 May 1952, by Plt Off Bill Simmonds.

55
Meteor F.Mk 8 A77-851 *"HALESTORM"*, flown by Sgt George Hale, No 77 Sqn
Hale scored his historic kill on 27 March 1953 during a strafing mission against targets on the Pyongyang-Singosan road. 'MiG killer' was scrawled in the carbon deposits around Hale's gun muzzles after the sortie.

56
MiG-15 925, flown by Col Yevgeni Pepelyaev, commander of the 196th IAP
Yevgeni Pepelyaev was the top-scoring fighter pilot of the Korean War, amassing his 23 victories in 108 combat missions. Pepelyaev commanded the most successful Soviet unit which participated in Korea, the 196th IAP. This was one of the two constituent regiments of the 324th Istrebeitel Aviatsionnaya Diviziya (Fighter Aviation Division) commanded by World War 2 ace Ivan Kozhedub.

FIGURE PLATES

1
A 25th FIS/51st FIW 1st Lieutenant in mid-1952, dressed in army fatigues and combat boots. The pilot is also wearing an old Army Air Force olive drab flying jacket with a USAAF patch printed on the sleeve. The badge of rank is worn on a squadron-coloured red baseball cap – these became very popular on the frontline bases as the war progressed. The 10th US ace of the war, Capt Iven Kincheloe, was photographed on several occasions wearing a uniform similar in many respects to this one.

2
Capt Manuel 'Pete' Fernandez in the spring of 1953, wearing the standard service cap for officers, regulation blue flying suit and thin summer issue flying jacket. He has personalised the latter by having a large 334th FIS 'boxing pigeon' patch sewn on to its left breast. Further confirming his allegiance to the 334th, Fernandez has an appropriately coloured scarf tied loosely around his neck. He is also wearing a battered pair of brogan boots (favoured, although unofficial, footwear in the summer months), whilst in his hands, Fernandez is holding his flying helmet and Mae West.

3
Capt Harold Fischer in late 1952 at Suwon. He is dressed in similar regulation issue clothing as shown on Pete Fernandez, but instead of an officer's service issue cap, he is wearing a garrison, or 'overseas', cap with captain's bars pinned on – the latter are also worn on the collars of his flying suit. Attached to the 39th FIS/51st FIW, Fischer has a distinctive yellow life jacket strapped to his chest, G-suit webbing around his lower waist and legs and a bulky parachute pack strapped to his back.

4
One of the last aces of the war, Maj John F Bolt was also the only Marine Corps pilot to achieve this distinction in three years of fighting, although he had to first be transferred to a Sabre unit to score the required kills. Assigned to the 39 FIS/51st FIW, Bolt still wore his USMC uniform whilst attached to the USAF – 'forest green' overalls and a Navy issue A-2 leather jacket

5
Col Yevgeni Pepelyaev, commander of the 196th IAP (Fighter Aviation Regiment), was the top scoring pilot of the Korean conflict. He is depicted here wearing a standard Soviet Air Force issue uniform that includes a leather flying jacket – pilots usually flew in all weathers clothed in this basic apparel as the cramped confines of the MiG-15's cockpit precluded the wearing of fur-lined suits. No distinguishing rank tabs or unit badges are visible, and his cap is very similar in style to the regulation Red Army officer's head gear.

6
Arguably the most famous British pilot of the Korean War was Lt Peter 'Hoagy' Carmichael, a modest Sea Fury FB.Mk 11 'driver' assigned to No 802 Sqn, embarked aboard HMS *Ocean* in mid-1952. He is wearing standard issue light blue, RAF style, overalls, with rank badges on the epaulettes, and a Mae West. Carmichael is clutching his 'bone-dome' in his hand, whilst on his head he is wearing his 'hats-electric' – a skull cap containing a headset which was thin enough to wear underneath the basic flying helmet of the period.